The roman Catholic Daily and
Sunday Missal 2024

Christopher amos

First edition

This book was professionally typeset on Reedsy.
Find out more at reedsy.com

Contents

VII Conclusion

I

Introduction

As you hold this Roman Catholic Daily and Sunday Missal 2024 in your hands, you are embarking on a journey of faith and prayer. This missal is not merely a book of liturgical texts; it is a companion for your spiritual life, guiding you through the rich tapestry of the liturgical year and deepening your encounter with Christ in the Eucharist

1

Purpose of the Missal

The purpose of this Missal is to guide Catholics in their partici- pation in the sacred liturgy, particularly in the celebration of the Mass. It serves as a valuable resource, providing the prayers, readings, and liturgical texts for both daily and Sunday Masses throughout the year.

The Missal helps the faithful to enter more deeply into the mysteries of the faith, allowing them to follow along with the prayers of the Mass and to meditate on the Word of God as it is proclaimed in the readings. Through the prayers of the Mass, we are united with Christ in his sacrifice on the cross and are nourished by his Body and Blood in the Eucharist.

The Missal also helps to foster a sense of unity among Catholics, as we pray the same prayers and hear the same readings at Mass, regardless of where we are in the world. This unity is a visible sign of the communion that we share as members of the Body of Christ.

Moreover, the Missal serves as a rich source of spiritual nourishment, providing prayers and devotions that can be used outside of Mass to deepen our relationship with God. These prayers help us to express our love for God, to seek his guidance and protection, and to offer him thanksgiving for the blessings we have received.

In using the Missal, we are following in the footsteps of the early Christians, who "devoted themselves to the apostles' teaching and fellowship, to the breaking of bread and the prayers" (Acts 2:42). Just as they relied on the apostles to teach them the faith and to lead them in prayer, so too do we rely on the Church's liturgical texts to guide us in our worship of God..

In conclusion, the Roman Catholic Daily and Sunday Missal is a precious gift to the Church, helping us to grow in our love for God and in our understanding of the mysteries of the faith. Through its prayers and readings, we are drawn closer to Christ and are strengthened to live out our faith in the world. May we always cherish this Missal and allow it to deepen our relationship with our Lord and Savior, Jesus Christ.

2

Importance of liturgy in Catholic Life

As we embark on this journey through the Roman Catholic Daily and Sunday Missal 2024, it is important to understand the profound significance of the liturgy in our Catholic life. The liturgy is not just a series of rituals and prayers; it is the very heart of our faith, the source and summit of our Christian existence (cf. **Catechism of the Catholic Church** 1324).

The Importance of the Liturgy in Catholic Life:

1. Encounter with God: The liturgy is where we encounter God in a profound and intimate way. Through the liturgical celebra- tions, especially the Holy Eucharist, we enter into communion with the Triune God—Father, Son, and Holy Spirit. It is in the liturgy that we experience God's presence, hear His word, and receive His grace.

    Biblical Example: In the Gospel of John, Jesus proclaims, "I am the bread of life. Whoever comes to me will never be hungry, and whoever believes in me will never be thirsty" (John 6:35). This verse highlights the central role of the Eucharist in our spiritual nourishment and communion with God.

2. Communal Worship: The liturgy is a communal act of worship where the Body of Christ, the Church, comes together to praise and thank God. It is a foretaste of the heavenly liturgy, where all the saints and angels worship God in unison.

Biblical Example: In the Book of Revelation, the Apostle John describes a vision of heavenly worship, where he sees a great multitude from every nation, tribe, people, and language standing before the throne of God, singing praises to Him (Revelation 7:9-10).

3. Source of Grace: The liturgy is a privileged source of grace for the faithful. Through the sacraments celebrated in the liturgy, especially the Eucharist and Reconciliation, we receive the grace necessary for our salvation and sanctification.

Biblical Example: In the Gospel of Matthew, Jesus institutes the sacrament of the Eucharist at the Last Supper, saying, "Take, eat; this is my body... Drink from it, all of you; for this is my blood of the covenant, which is poured out for many for the forgiveness of sins" (Matthew 26:26-28).

4. Formation and Transformation: The liturgy forms and transforms us as Christians. Through active participation in the liturgical celebrations, we are shaped into the image of Christ and empowered to live out our faith in the world.

Biblical Example: St. Paul writes to the Romans, "Do not be conformed to this world, but be transformed by the renewing of your minds, so that you may discern what is the will of God — what is good and acceptable and perfect" (Romans 12:2). This transformation happens through our active engagement with the liturgy.

5. Unity and Communion: The liturgy fosters unity and communion among believers. It reminds us that we are one body in Christ, called to love and serve one another in imitation of Him.

Biblical Example: St. Paul, in his First Letter to the Corinthians, writes about the unity of the Church, saying, "For in the one Spirit we were all baptized into one body—Jews or Greeks, slaves or free—and we were all made to drink of one Spirit" (1 Corinthians 12:13).

In conclusion, the liturgy is not just an obligation or a routine; it is a sacred and transformative encounter with the living God. May our participation in the liturgy deepen our faith, strengthen our communion with God and one another, and empower us to be faithful witnesses of the Gospel in the world.

3

How to Use This Missal

As you hold this Roman Catholic Daily and Sunday Missal 2024 in your hands, you are embarking on a journey of faith and prayer. This missal is not merely a book of liturgical texts; it is a companion for your spiritual life, guiding you through the rich tapestry of the liturgical year and deepening your encounter with Christ in the Eucharist.

How to Use This Missal

    1. Understanding the Liturgical Year: The liturgical year is the Church's way of celebrating and commemorating the life, death, and resurrection of Jesus Christ. It is divided into seasons, each with its own theme and focus. For example, Advent is a season of preparation and anticipation, while Lent is a time of repentance and spiritual renewal. The missal provides readings, prayers, and reflections specific to each season, helping you to enter more fully into the mystery of Christ's saving work.

    Biblical Example: In Luke 4:16-21, Jesus reads from the scroll of the prophet Isaiah, proclaiming that the Spirit of the

Lord is upon Him to bring good news to the poor and freedom to the captives. This passage highlights Jesus' mission and sets the tone for the Church's mission during Advent and throughout the year.

2. Navigating the Mass: The missal contains all the prayers and readings for both daily and Sunday Masses. It includes the Order of Mass, which outlines the structure of the liturgy, as well as the Proper of Seasons, which provides the prayers and readings specific to each day of the liturgical year. Familiarize yourself with these sections to follow along and participate more fully in the Mass.

Biblical Example: In 1 Corinthians 11:23-26, St. Paul recounts the words of Jesus at the Last Supper, instituting the Eucharist. This passage reminds us of the central importance of the Eucharist in the life of the Church and encourages us to approach the Mass with reverence and devotion.

3. Praying with the Church: The missal invites you to unite your prayers with those of the Church throughout the world and across the centuries. By following the prayers and readings prescribed by the Church, you join in the universal prayer of the Body of Christ, lifting up your intentions and those of the whole world to God.

Biblical Example: In Acts 2:42, we read that the early Christian community devoted themselves to the apostles' teaching, fellowship, the breaking of bread, and prayer. This passage shows us the importance of communal prayer and worship in the life of the Church.

4. Deepening Your Spiritual Life: As you use this missal,

allow it to deepen your relationship with Christ. Reflect on the readings and prayers, allowing them to speak to your heart and guide you in your daily life. Use the missal as a tool for personal prayer and reflection, allowing the Word of God to transform you from within.

Biblical Example: In Psalm 119:105, the psalmist declares, "Your word is a lamp to my feet and a light to my path." This verse reminds us that God's Word is a guide for our lives, leading us on the path of righteousness.

In conclusion, dear friends, may this Roman Catholic Daily and Sunday Missal 2024 be a source of grace and blessing to you as you journey through the liturgical year. May it deepen your love for Christ and His Church, and may it inspire you to live your faith more fully each day.

II

Liturgical year

The liturgical year is a sacred and cyclical journey that guides us through the life, death, and resurrection of Jesus Christ. It is a rich tapestry of seasons, feasts, and solemnities that deepen our faith and draw us closer to God. As a Catholic priest, I am deeply invested in the liturgical year, as it forms the backbone of our worship and spiritual life.

4

Advent

Advent is a season of joyful anticipation and preparation for the celebration of the birth of Jesus Christ at Christmas. The word "Advent" comes from the Latin word "adventus," which means "coming" or "arrival." It is a time when we, as Christians, reflect on the first coming of Jesus in Bethlehem over two thousand years ago and also look forward to his second coming at the end of time.

The Advent season begins on the fourth Sunday before Christmas, which is known as Advent Sunday. This year, it falls on November 29th. The season lasts for four weeks, leading up to Christmas Eve. During this time, we prepare ourselves spiritually for the coming of Christ by focusing on themes of hope, peace, joy, and love.

The Advent wreath is a common symbol of this season. It typically consists of a wreath with four candles, three purple and one pink, arranged around the wreath. Each Sunday of Advent, one more candle is lit, symbolizing the increasing light

13

of Christ coming into the world.

The color purple is used in Advent to symbolize penance, preparation, and royalty. It reminds us to prepare our hearts and minds for the coming of Christ, who is the King of Kings. The third Sunday of Advent is known as Gaudete Sunday, from the Latin word "gaudete," which means "rejoice." On this Sunday, the pink candle is lit, symbolizing our joy in anticipation of the coming of Christ.

Throughout Advent, we are called to reflect on the prophecies of the Old Testament that foretold the coming of the Messiah. For example, Isaiah 7:14 says, "Therefore the Lord himself will give you a sign: The virgin will conceive and give birth to a son, and will call him Immanuel." This prophecy was fulfilled in the birth of Jesus, who was born of the Virgin Mary.

Advent is also a time of spiritual preparation, where we are called to examine our lives and repent of our sins. It is a time of prayer, fasting, and almsgiving, as we prepare ourselves to welcome Christ into our hearts and homes. It is a time to focus on the true meaning of Christmas, which is not about material gifts or holiday festivities, but about the gift of God's love and salvation through his Son, Jesus Christ.

As we journey through the season of Advent, let us take to heart the words of Isaiah 9:6, "For to us a child is born, to us a son is given, and the government will be on his shoulders. And he will be called Wonderful Counselor, Mighty God, Everlasting Father, Prince of Peace." Let us prepare ourselves to welcome the Prince of Peace into our lives and hearts this Advent season.

5

Significance of Advent

The significance of Advent lies in its dual nature. On one hand, it is a time of joyful anticipation and celebration as we prepare to celebrate the birth of Jesus, the long-awaited Messiah, who came to save humanity from sin and reconcile us with God. The birth of Jesus is a pivotal moment in salvation history, and Advent allows us to reflect on the profound mystery of the Incarnation, the Son of God becoming human.

On the other hand, Advent is also a time of penance and reflection, reminding us of the need for spiritual preparation for the coming of Christ. Just as the people of Israel waited for the coming of the Messiah, so too do we wait for the second coming of Christ at the end of time. Advent calls us to examine our lives, repent of our sins, and prepare our hearts to receive Christ both at Christmas and at the end of time.

Biblical Examples:
  - Isaiah 9:6-7: "For to us a child is born, to us a son is given, and the government will be on his shoulders. And he will be

called Wonderful Counselor, Mighty God, Everlasting Father, Prince of Peace. Of the greatness of his government and peace there will be no end. He will reign on David's throne and over his kingdom, establishing and upholding it with justice and righteousness from that time on and forever. The zeal of the Lord Almighty will accomplish this."

- Matthew 24:44: "So you also must be ready, because the Son of Man will come at an hour when you do not expect him." - Luke 1:26-38: The Annunciation, when the angel Gabriel announces to Mary that she will conceive and bear a son, Jesus, who will be the Son of God. This event marks the beginning of the Incarnation and the fulfillment of God's promise to send a Savior.

In summary, Advent is a season of joyful anticipation and penitential preparation as we await the celebration of the birth of Jesus at Christmas and prepare for his second coming. It is a time to reflect on the meaning of Christ's birth and its significance for our lives, as well as to prepare our hearts to receive him both now and in the future.

6

Advent Traditions and Practices

Advent, derived from the Latin word "adventus," meaning "coming," is a season of joyful expectation and preparation for the celebration of the birth of Jesus Christ at Christmas and the anticipation of his second coming. It is a time marked by a sense of hope, longing, and waiting. During Advent, Catholics engage in various traditions and practices that help deepen their spiritual awareness and prepare their hearts to receive the Christ Child.

1. **Advent Wreath:** One of the most popular Advent traditions is the Advent wreath. The wreath is typically made of evergreen branches, symbolizing eternal life, and is adorned with four candles, three purple and one rose or pink. Each candle represents a different aspect of the Advent journey. The first candle, usually lit on the first Sunday of Advent, symbolizes hope. The second candle, lit on the second Sunday, symbolizes peace. The third candle, often called the "Gaudete Sunday" candle, symbolizes joy and is lit on the third Sunday of Advent. The fourth candle represents love and is lit on the fourth Sunday

of Advent.

Biblical Example: The lighting of candles symbolizes the increasing light of Christ coming into the world. As John 1:5 (NIV) states, "The light shines in the darkness, and the darkness has not overcome it."

2. Advent Calendar: Another popular Advent tradition is the Advent calendar. This is a special calendar used to count down the days of Advent in anticipation of Christmas. Each day, a door or window is opened to reveal a picture, a Bible verse, or a small gift, helping to build excitement and focus on the true meaning of Christmas.

Biblical Example: The concept of counting down to an important event is seen in the Old Testament with the Israelites eagerly awaiting the coming of the Messiah. Isaiah 9:6 (NIV) prophesies, "For to us a child is born, to us a son is given, and the government will be on his shoulders. And he will be called Wonderful Counselor, Mighty God, Everlasting Father, Prince of Peace."

3. Advent Fasting and Prayer: Advent is also a time of spiritual preparation through fasting and prayer. Catholics are encouraged to use this time to reflect on their lives, repent of their sins, and turn their hearts toward God. This practice helps to cultivate a spirit of humility and dependence on God's grace.

Biblical Example: Fasting and prayer are seen throughout the Bible as ways to draw closer to God and seek His will. In Matthew 6:16-18 (NIV), Jesus teaches about fasting: "When you fast, do not look somber as the hypocrites do, for they disfigure their faces to show others they are fasting. Truly I tell you, they have received their reward in full. But when you fast, put oil on your head and wash your face, so that it will not be obvious to others that you are fasting, but only to your Father, who is unseen; and your Father, who sees what is done in secret, will reward you."

4. Advent Confession: Many Catholics also take the opportunity to participate in the sacrament of confession during Advent. Confession allows individuals to receive God's forgiveness for their sins and to experience spiritual renewal as they prepare to welcome the Savior into their hearts.

Biblical Example: Confession is rooted in the teachings of Jesus, who gave His apostles the authority to forgive sins. In John 20:22-23 (NIV), Jesus says to His disciples, "Receive the Holy Spirit. If you forgive anyone's sins, their sins are forgiven; if you do not forgive them, they are not forgiven."

5. Advent Acts of Charity: Advent is a season of giving and serving others, mirroring God's ultimate gift of His Son to humanity. Catholics are encouraged to perform acts of charity and kindness, such as visiting the sick, feeding the hungry, and clothing the naked, as a way of preparing their hearts to receive Christ.

Biblical Example: Jesus teaches the importance of charity in Matthew 25:35-36 (NIV): "For I was hungry and you gave me something to eat, I was thirsty and you gave me something to drink, I was a stranger and you invited me in, I needed clothes and you clothed me, I was sick and you looked after me, I was in prison and you came to visit me."

7

Liturgical Readings and Prayers for Advent

As we approach the season of Advent, the Church invites us to embark on a spiritual journey of preparation and anticipation. Advent, which comes from the Latin word "adventus," meaning "coming," is a time of waiting and preparing for the coming of Christ. It is a season of hope and expectation, as we await the celebration of the birth of Jesus at Christmas and look forward to his second coming at the end of time.

The liturgical readings and prayers for Advent are carefully selected to help us enter more deeply into the mystery of Christ's coming. They are meant to inspire us, challenge us, and guide us as we prepare our hearts to welcome the Lord into our lives. Let us explore these readings and prayers in more detail, reflecting on their significance and relevance to our lives today.

1. **The Prophecies of the Messiah**: The readings during Advent often focus on the prophecies of the Messiah found

in the Old Testament. These prophecies, such as those found in Isaiah, remind us of God's promise to send a savior to redeem his people. For example, Isaiah 7:14 prophesies, "Therefore the Lord himself will give you a sign: The virgin will conceive and give birth to a son, and will call him Immanuel." This verse foreshadows the birth of Jesus, who is the fulfillment of God's promise to send a savior.

2. **John the Baptist and the Call to Repentance**: Another theme of Advent is the role of John the Baptist, who prepared the way for Jesus. John's message of repentance reminds us of the importance of preparing our hearts for the coming of Christ. As John proclaimed in Matthew 3:2, "Repent, for the kingdom of heaven has come near." During Advent, we are called to examine our lives, repent of our sins, and make room for Christ in our hearts.

3. **The Annunciation**: The story of the Annunciation, when the angel Gabriel announced to Mary that she would conceive and bear a son, is also often read during Advent. This story reminds us of Mary's faith and willingness to cooperate with God's plan. It challenges us to be open to God's will in our own lives, just as Mary was. As Mary said in Luke 1:38, "I am the Lord's servant. May your word to me be fulfilled."

4. **The Second Coming of Christ**: While Advent is a time of preparing for the celebration of Christ's birth, it is also a time of looking forward to his second coming. The readings during Advent remind us that we are called to be vigilant and prepared for the day when Christ will come again. As Jesus said in Matthew 24:44, "So you also must be ready, because the Son of Man will come at an hour

when you do not expect him."

5. **Prayers of Hope and Expectation**: Along side the readings, the prayers of the Advent season express our hope and expectation of Christ's coming. These prayers often reflect themes of longing, waiting, and anticipation. For example, the Advent hymn "O Come, O Come, Emmanuel" expresses the longing of God's people for the coming of
the Messiah.

As we journey through the season of Advent, may we be inspired by the liturgical readings and prayers to prepare our hearts to welcome Christ into our lives. May we be like Mary, who said "yes" to God's plan with faith and humility. And may we be vigilant and prepared for the day when Christ will come again, bringing with him the fulfillment of God's kingdom.

Christmas

Christmas is a central feast in the liturgical year of the Catholic Church, celebrating the birth of Jesus Christ, the Son of God, into the world. It is a time of great joy and hope, as we remember and reflect on the incarnation of God's love for humanity. The word "Christmas" itself comes from the Old English "Cristes Maesse," meaning the Mass of Christ, highlighting the religious significance of the day.

10

Celebration of the Nativity

As we delve into the role of the Christmas season, we are called to contemplate the profound mystery of the Nativity —the birth of our Lord and Savior, Jesus Christ. This celebration, which marks the incarnation of God's divine Son, is a central tenet of our faith, embodying the essence of God's love and mercy for humanity.

The Nativity story, as recounted in the Gospels of Matthew and Luke, provides us with a glimpse into the humble circumstances surrounding the birth of Jesus. Born in Bethlehem, a small town in Judea, Jesus was born to Mary, a young virgin, and Joseph, a carpenter. Despite their humble origins, the birth of Jesus was nothing short of miraculous, as it fulfilled the prophecies of the Old Testament regarding the coming of the Messiah.

The Gospel of Luke offers a detailed account of the Nativity, describing how Mary and Joseph traveled to Bethlehem for the census decreed by Caesar Augustus. Unable to find lodging in the overcrowded town, they sought shelter in a stable, where Mary gave birth to Jesus. This humble setting, with its manger and animals, underscores the humility and simplicity of Jesus' birth, emphasizing his identification with the poor and marginalized.

The birth of Jesus was accompanied by extraordinary signs and wonders. According to the Gospel of Matthew, a star appeared in the sky, guiding the Magi, or Wise Men, to the place where Jesus lay. These Wise Men, representing the Gentile nations, came to pay homage to the newborn King, bearing gifts of gold, frankincense, and myrrh. Their presence at the Nativity highlights the universal significance of Jesus' birth, foreshadowing his mission to bring salvation to all people, regardless of their background or status.

The Nativity also holds deep theological significance for Chris- tians. It represents the fulfillment of God's promise to send a savior to redeem humanity from sin and death. As the Gospel of John proclaims, "The Word became flesh and made his dwelling among us" (John 1:14). In Jesus, the eternal Son of God took on human nature, entering into our world to share in our joys and sorrows, and ultimately to offer himself as a sacrifice for our sins.

The Nativity invites us to reflect on the true meaning of Christ- mas. It is not merely a time for festive celebrations and gift- giving, but a solemn occasion to contemplate the mystery of God's love made manifest in the birth of Jesus. As we gather with family and friends to celebrate this joyous season, let us remember the true reason for our joy—the birth of our Savior, who came to bring us salvation and eternal life.

In conclusion, the celebration of the Nativity is a profound reminder of God's love and mercy for humanity. It invites us to contemplate the mystery of the Incarnation and to deepen our faith in the saving power of Jesus Christ. As we celebrate this Christmas season, may we be filled with gratitude for the gift of our Savior and may we strive to imitate his love and compassion in our lives.

11

The Twelve Days of Christmas

In the Catholic tradition, the Twelve Days of Christmas are a time of celebration and reflection that begin on December 25th and end on January 5th, the eve of the Feast of the Epiphany. This period is also known as Christmastide or the Christmas season, and it is a time to joyfully commemorate the birth of Jesus Christ.

During these twelve days, Catholics are encouraged to deepen their understanding of the mystery of the Incarnation—the belief that God became human in the person of Jesus Christ. This central doctrine of the Christian faith is a profound expression of God's love for humanity, as described in John 3:16: "For God so loved the world that he gave his only Son, so that everyone who believes in him might not perish but might have eternal life."

The Twelve Days of Christmas are not only a time of celebration but also a time of spiritual renewal and growth. Catholics are invited to reflect on the significance of Christ's birth and its implications for their lives. This period offers an opportunity to meditate on the humility and love of God as demonstrated in the person of Jesus Christ, who "though he was in the form of God, did not regard equality with God something to be grasped. Rather, he emptied himself, taking the form of a slave, coming in human likeness" (Philippians 2:6-7).

Liturgically, the Twelve Days of Christmas are marked by special readings and prayers that focus on the various aspects of the Christmas story. The readings typically include passages from the Gospels of Matthew and Luke, which recount the events surrounding the birth of Jesus, as well as reflections on the significance of his coming for the salvation of humanity.

One of the key themes of the Christmas season is the idea of light coming into the world. This motif is central to the Gospel of John, which describes Jesus as the "light of the world" (John 8:12) and emphasizes the role of faith in receiving this light: "But to all who received him, who believed in his name, he gave power to become children of God" (John 1:12).

In addition to the readings, the liturgical prayers for Christmas emphasize the themes of joy, peace, and hope that are associated with the birth of Jesus. These prayers often express gratitude for the gift of salvation that has come into the world through Christ and invoke God's blessings on all people.

Overall, the Twelve Days of Christmas are a time of spiritual renewal and reflection for Catholics. They offer an opportunity to deepen one's faith and to reflect on the profound mystery of the Incarnation. As we celebrate the birth of Jesus Christ, let us remember the words of the prophet Isaiah: "For a child is born to us, a son is given to us; upon his shoulder dominion rests. They name him Wonder-Counselor, God-Hero, Father-Forever, Prince of Peace" (Isaiah 9:5).

12

Liturgical Readings and Prayers for Christmas

Christmas is a joyous celebration in the Catholic liturgical calendar, marking the birth of Jesus Christ, our Savior. The readings and prayers for Christmas Masses are carefully selected to reflect the significance of this event in salvation history and to inspire the faithful to deepen their understanding and appreciation of God's great gift to humanity.

The liturgical readings for Christmas typically include the following:

1. Vigil Mass:
     - The Vigil Mass readings often focus on the anticipation and preparation for the birth of Christ. The first reading may come from the Book of Isaiah, prophesying the coming of the Messiah, such as Isaiah 9:1-6, which foretells the birth of a child who will bring light and joy to the people.

   - The Gospel reading usually narrates the genealogy of Jesus or the Annunciation to Mary, highlighting the fulfillment of God's promise to send a Savior. For example, the Gospel of Matthew 1:18-25 tells the story of the angel Gabriel appearing to Joseph in a dream to announce the birth of Jesus.

2. Midnight Mass:

- The Midnight Mass readings emphasize the mystery and wonder of the Incarnation. The first reading often comes from the Book of Isaiah, such as Isaiah 62:1-5, which speaks of God's everlasting love for His people and the coming of salvation.

- The Gospel reading at Midnight Mass is the Nativity story itself, taken from the Gospel of Luke 2:1-14, describing the birth of Jesus in Bethlehem, the angel's announcement to the shepherds, and the heavenly host praising God.

3. Mass at Dawn:

- The Mass at Dawn readings focus on the shepherds' visit to the manger and the revelation of Christ's birth to them. The first reading may be from the Prophet Isaiah, such as Isaiah 62:11-12, which proclaims the arrival of the Redeemer and the call to proclaim His salvation to all nations.

- The Gospel reading continues the Nativity story, often from the Gospel of Luke 2:15-20, where the shepherds visit the newborn Jesus and glorify God for what they have seen and heard.

4. Mass during the Day:

- The Mass during the Day readings deepen our understanding of the Incarnation and its significance for humanity. The first reading may be from the Prophet Isaiah, such as Isaiah

52:7-10, which announces the reign of God and the salvation He brings.

- The Gospel reading at Mass during the Day is from the begin- ning of the Gospel of John (John 1:1-18), known as the Prologue, which proclaims the Word becoming flesh and dwelling among us, revealing God's glory and truth.

The prayers for Christmas Masses reflect the themes of joy, hope, peace, and salvation that accompany the birth of Christ. They invite the faithful to contemplate the mystery of the Incarnation and to respond with faith and gratitude. The prayers often include expressions of praise and thanksgiving to God for His gift of love and mercy.

One of the most well-known prayers for Christmas is the Collect, or Opening Prayer, which is different for each Mass. An example of a Collect for Christmas Day is:
"O God, who wonderfully created the dignity of human nature and still more wonderfully restored it, grant, we pray, that we may share in the divinity of Christ, who humbled himself to share in our humanity. Who lives and reigns with you in the unity of the Holy Spirit, one God, for ever and ever. Amen."

This prayer acknowledges the greatness of God's gift in sending His Son to become human, restoring our dignity and offering us a share in His divine life. It echoes the words of St. Paul in Philippians 2:6-7, where he describes Christ's humility in taking on human form for our salvation.

In conclusion, the liturgical readings and prayers for Christmas

Masses are rich in meaning and significance, inviting us to enter more deeply into the mystery of the Incarnation and to rejoice in the gift of God's Son. They remind us of God's great love for us and His desire to be with us, Emmanuel, "God with us." May this Christmas season be a time of renewed faith, hope, and love as we celebrate the birth of our Savior, Jesus Christ.

14

Ordinary Time I,

Ordinary Time is a significant and unique season in the liturgical calendar of the Catholic Church. It is a time of growth, reflection, and living out the teachings of Christ in our daily lives. The term "Ordinary" in Ordinary Time does not mean common or mundane; rather, it comes from the Latin word "ordinalis," which means "numbered." Ordinary Time is called so because the weeks are numbered (e.g., the 1st week of Ordinary Time, the 2nd week, and so on), not because it is unimportant.

One of the key aspects of Ordinary Time is its focus on the life and teachings of Jesus Christ. During this season, the Church reflects on the ministry of Jesus as recorded in the Gospels. It is a time to delve deeply into the words and actions of Jesus, to learn from His teachings, and to apply them to our lives.

A central theme of Ordinary Time is discipleship. Just as Jesus called His disciples to follow Him, Ordinary Time calls us to deepen our commitment to Christ and His teachings. It is a time for us to reflect on what it means to be a disciple of Jesus and how we can live out our faith in our daily lives.

One of the key aspects of Ordinary Time is its focus on growth and maturation in faith. Just as the natural seasons of the year bring growth and change, so too does Ordinary Time bring opportunities for spiritual growth and transformation. It is a time for us to deepen our relationship with God and to grow in our understanding of His will for our lives.

During Ordinary Time, the liturgical color is green, symbolizing hope and growth. Green is the color of life and renewal, reminding us of the evergreen trees that remain vibrant and alive even in the midst of winter. This color serves as a visual reminder of the new life and growth that God desires for each of us during this season.

In the Gospels, we see many examples of Jesus teaching His disciples during Ordinary Time. One such example is found in the Gospel of Mark, where Jesus teaches His disciples about the Kingdom of God through parables. In Mark 4:26-29, Jesus tells the parable of the growing seed, illustrating how the Kingdom of God grows and develops unseen, much like the growth that occurs in our own spiritual lives during Ordinary Time.

Overall, Ordinary Time is a season of growth, reflection, and discipleship. It is a time for us to deepen our relationship with God, to learn from the teachings of Jesus, and to grow in our faith. As we journey through Ordinary Time, may we be open to the work of the Holy Spirit in our lives, guiding us and transforming us into faithful disciples of Christ.

15

Lent

Dear believers approach the sacred season of Lent, we are invited to embark on a profound journey of spiritual renewal and growth. Lent is a time of reflection, repentance, and preparation for the joyous celebration of Easter. It is a season in which we are called to deepen our relationship with God, to turn away from sin, and to embrace the transformative power of His love and mercy.

1. Understanding the Meaning of Lent:

Lent derives its name from the Old English word "lencten," which means "springtime." Just as spring is a season of new life and growth in nature, Lent is a spiritual springtime in which we are called to renew our hearts and minds. Lent lasts for forty days, symbolizing the forty days Jesus spent in the desert fasting and praying before beginning His public ministry

(Matthew 4:1-11).

During Lent, we are called to imitate Jesus by entering into a period of self-examination, repentance, and self-denial. It is a time to confront our own weaknesses and shortcomings, to seek forgiveness for our sins, and to make a sincere effort to amend our lives. Lent is not simply a time of giving up things; it is a time of drawing closer to God and allowing His grace to transform us from within.

2. Practices and Traditions of Lent:

a. Prayer: Prayer is the foundation of our Lenten journey. Through prayer, we communicate with God, deepen our rela- tionship with Him, and open our hearts to His will. During Lent, we are encouraged to dedicate more time to prayer, both individually and as a community. We can pray the Liturgy of the Hours, meditate on Scripture, participate in Eucharistic adoration, and engage in personal prayer practices such as lectio divina or the rosary.

b. Fasting: Fasting is another essential aspect of Lent. By fasting, we discipline our bodies and detach ourselves from the distractions of the world, allowing us to focus more fully on God. Fasting reminds us of our dependence on God for all things and helps us to cultivate a spirit of humility and self-control. In the Bible, Jesus Himself fasted for forty days in the desert as a preparation for His ministry (Matthew 4:2). During Lent, Catholics are called to observe fasting and abstinence on Ash Wednesday and Good Friday, as well as to abstain from meat on Fridays throughout the season.

c. Almsgiving: Almsgiving is the practice of giving to those in need, following the example of Jesus who showed compassion and generosity to the poor and marginalized. During Lent, we are called to be mindful of the needs of others and to share our blessings with them. This may involve donating to charitable organizations, volunteering our time and talents, or reaching out to those who are lonely or suffering. As Jesus taught, "Truly I tell you, whatever you did for one of the least of these brothers and sisters of mine, you did for me" (Matthew 25:40).

d. Sacrament of Reconciliation: The Sacrament of Reconciliation, also known as Confession, is a central part of the Lenten journey. It offers us the opportunity to acknowledge our sins, receive God's forgiveness, and experience the healing grace of His love. Through the sacrament, we are reconciled with God and with one another, restoring our relationship with Him and with the Church. As St. Paul reminds us, "So if anyone is in Christ, there is a new creation: everything old has passed away; see, everything has become new!" (2 Corinthians 5:17).

3. Liturgical Readings and Prayers for Lent:

Throughout the season of Lent, the Church provides us with a rich array of liturgical readings and prayers that reflect the themes of repentance, redemption, and renewal. These readings guide us on our spiritual journey and invite us to meditate on the saving mysteries of Christ's passion, death, and resurrection. We are called to listen attentively to God's word, allowing it to penetrate our hearts and transform our lives. As the psalmist proclaims, "Your word is a lamp to my feet and a light to my path" (Psalm 119:105).

Conclusion:

My dear friends, as we enter into the season of Lent, let us embrace this sacred time with open hearts and minds. Let us commit ourselves to prayer, fasting, and almsgiving, seeking to draw closer to God and to grow in holiness. May this season be a time of profound spiritual renewal and transformation for each one of us, as we journey together toward the joy of Easter and the promise of new life in Christ.

16

Understanding Ordinary Time in the Liturgical Calendar

In the Roman Catholic liturgical calendar, Ordinary Time is a period of the liturgical year that is not part of the major seasons such as Advent, Christmas, Lent, or Easter. It is called "ordinary" not because it is unimportant, but because the weeks are numbered in sequence (e.g., the 1st Sunday in Ordinary Time, the 2nd Sunday in Ordinary Time, and so on). Ordinary Time is divided into two segments: one following the Christmas season and the other following the Easter season. Each segment highlights different aspects of the Christian life and faith.

The Symbolism of Green

The liturgical color for Ordinary Time is green, symbolizing hope and growth. This color reminds us of the ongoing growth and development of our faith as we journey through life. Just as green is the color of plants that continue to grow and bear fruit, so too should our faith continue to grow and bear fruit in good works (Colossians 1:10).

The Purpose of Ordinary Time

Ordinary Time serves as a time of reflection and growth in our Christian discipleship. It is a time to reflect on the teachings of Jesus and how we can live out those teachings in our daily lives. It is a time to deepen our relationship with God and with one another, and to grow in faith, hope, and love.

The Readings and Themes of Ordinary Time

The readings during Ordinary Time focus on the teachings and miracles of Jesus, as well as other passages from the Bible that highlight key aspects of Christian faith and life. These readings challenge us to live out our faith in concrete ways and to be witnesses to the Gospel in the world.

Living in Ordinary Time

Living in Ordinary Time means living our faith in the ordinary moments of our daily lives. It means being attentive to the presence of God in our midst and responding to God's grace with generosity and love. It means being open to the opportunities for growth and transformation that God presents to us each day.

Biblical Examples of Ordinary Time

One biblical example of living in Ordinary Time is the story of the disciples on the road to Emmaus (Luke 24:13-35). In this story, two disciples encounter the risen Jesus on the road, but they do not recognize him at first. It is only through their conversation with Jesus and the breaking of the bread that their eyes are opened and they recognize him. This story reminds us that Jesus is present with us in the ordinary moments of our

43

lives, and that we can encounter him in unexpected ways.

Another biblical example is the story of Jesus' encounter with the Samaritan woman at the well (John 4:1-42). In this story, Je- sus meets the woman at a well and engages her in conversation, revealing to her his true identity as the Messiah. This encounter transforms the woman's life and leads her to become a witness to Jesus in her community. This story reminds us that God can work through ordinary encounters and everyday situations to bring about extraordinary change in our lives and in the world.

Conclusion

In conclusion, Ordinary Time is a rich and meaningful season in the liturgical calendar. It is a time for us to grow in our relationship with God and to deepen our understanding of our faith. It is a time to be attentive to God's presence in our lives and to respond to God's grace with generosity and love. May we embrace the opportunities for growth and transformation that God presents to us during this season, and may we be witnesses to the Gospel in all that we do.

17

Liturgical Readings and Prayers for Lent

During the season of Lent, the Catholic Church invites believers to embark on a journey of spiritual renewal and transformation. This season is a time of prayer, fasting, and almsgiving, all aimed at deepening our relationship with God and preparing our hearts for the celebration of Easter. The liturgical readings and prayers for Lent are carefully chosen to reflect the themes of repentance, conversion, and the mercy of God.

1. Ash Wednesday
- Reading: Joel 2:12-18
- This passage from the prophet Joel calls the people to repentance, fasting, and mourning for their sins. It emphasizes the mercy and compassion of God, who is ready to forgive those who return to him with all their hearts.
- Prayer: Psalm 51:3-4, 12-13, 17
- This psalm is a beautiful expression of contrition and a plea for God's mercy. It acknowledges the reality of sin and asks God to create a clean heart and renew a right spirit within us.

2. First Sunday of Lent

- Reading: Luke 4:1-13
- The Gospel reading recounts Jesus' temptation in the desert, where he fasted for forty days and was tempted by the devil. It reminds us of the importance of resisting temptation and relying on God's word.
- Prayer: Psalm 91:1-2, 9-16
    - This psalm speaks of God's protection and care for those who trust in him. It encourages us to seek refuge in God and not to fear, even in the face of temptation.

3. Second Sunday of Lent

- Reading: Genesis 15:5-12, 17-18
    - In this reading, God makes a covenant with Abraham, promising him descendants as numerous as the stars. It is a reminder of God's faithfulness and the fulfillment of his promises.
- Prayer: Psalm 27:1, 7-9, 13-14
    - This psalm expresses confidence in God's protection and salvation. It encourages us to wait patiently for the Lord and to be strong and take heart.

4. Third Sunday of Lent

- Reading: Exodus 17:3-7
    - The reading recounts the Israelites' grumbling and lack of faith in the desert, and God's provision of water from the rock. It reminds us of the importance of trusting in God's provision.
- Prayer: Psalm 95:1-2, 6-9
    - This psalm calls us to worship and bow down before the Lord, our Maker. It warns against hardening our hearts and testing God as the Israelites did.

5. Fourth Sunday of Lent (Laetare Sunday)

- Reading: 2 Corinthians 5:17-21
  - This reading speaks of reconciliation with God through Christ and the ministry of reconciliation entrusted to us. It reminds us of the new life we have in Christ.
- Prayer: Psalm 34:6-7, 9-10, 13-14
  - This psalm praises God for his deliverance and invites us to taste and see that the Lord is good. It encourages us to fear the Lord and seek peace.

6. Fifth Sunday of Lent

- Reading: John 8:1-11
- The Gospel reading recounts the story of the woman caught in adultery and Jesus' mercy and forgiveness toward her. It reminds us of God's compassion and the call to repentance.
- Prayer: Psalm 126:1-6
  - This psalm praises God for his restoration of fortunes and expresses the joy of those who sow in tears but reap with shouts of joy. It encourages us to trust in God's faithfulness.

7. Palm Sunday

- Reading: Matthew 21:1-11 (Gospel)
- This reading recounts Jesus' triumphal entry into Jerusalem, where he is hailed as the Son of David. It foreshadows his passion and death.
- Prayer: Psalm 22:8-9, 17-20, 23-24
  - This psalm is a cry of anguish and a plea for deliverance. It anticipates the suffering and death of the righteous one, who ultimately trusts in God's salvation.

These readings and prayers for Lent guide us on our Lenten

journey, reminding us of the need for repentance, the reality of God's mercy, and the hope of new life in Christ. They encourage us to turn away from sin, trust in God's promises, and prepare our hearts to celebrate the joy of Easter.

18

Liturgical Readings and Prayers for Ordinary Time I

During Ordinary Time I, the Church enters a period of growth and reflection on the teachings of Christ. This season is marked by its green liturgical color, symbolizing hope and the continual growth of faith. The readings and prayers for Ordinary Time I focus on various aspects of Christian life and discipleship, drawing from the rich tapestry of biblical texts that guide and inspire believers.

1. **First Reading (Old Testament):** The Old Testament readings during Ordinary Time I often highlight themes of God's covenant with His people and the call to faithfulness. For example, the story of Noah and the flood (Genesis 6-9) demonstrates God's faithfulness to His promises and His desire for humanity to live in righteousness. This story reminds us of the importance of obedience to God's will.

2. **Responsorial Psalm:** The psalms chosen for Ordinary Time I resonate with themes of praise, thanksgiving, and trust in God's providence. Psalm 23, "The Lord is my

shepherd," is a comforting reminder of God's care and guidance in our lives. It reflects the idea of God as a loving shepherd who leads and protects His flock.

3. **Second Reading (New Testament)**: The New Testament readings during this time often focus on the teachings of Jesus and the apostles, emphasizing the call to live a life worthy of the Gospel. For example, in the letter of Paul to the Romans, we are reminded of our need to present our bodies as a living sacrifice, holy and pleasing to God (Romans 12:1-2). This passage challenges us to live lives of holiness and dedication to God.

4. **Gospel Reading**: The Gospel readings in Ordinary Time I present us with the life and teachings of Jesus, inviting us to deepen our relationship with Him. For example, the story of Jesus' baptism (Mark 1:9-11) reminds us of our own baptismal call to follow Christ. It symbolizes our dying to sin and rising to new life in Him.

5. **Prayers of the Faithful**: The prayers of the faithful in Ordinary Time I often reflect the themes of the readings, focusing on the needs of the Church and the world. These prayers offer intercession for the Church, the government, the sick, and those in need, aligning our hearts with God's will for the world.

In summary, Ordinary Time I is a season of growth and reflection, marked by its emphasis on living a life of faithfulness and discipleship. The readings and prayers for this time remind us of God's covenant love, our call to holiness, and the importance of living out our faith in our daily lives. As we journey through Ordinary Time I, may we be inspired by the example of Christ and His teachings, striving to live as faithful disciples in the world

20

Easter Triduum

The Easter Triduum is the three-day period that commemorates the passion, death, and resurrection of Jesus Christ. It is a time of intense reflection and prayer for Catholics around the world, culminating in the celebration of Easter Sunday. Each day of the Triduum has its own significance and rituals, starting with Holy Thursday.

Holy Thursday, also known as Maundy Thursday, marks the beginning of the Easter Triduum. It commemorates the Last Supper of Jesus with his disciples, where he instituted the sacraments of the Eucharist and the priesthood. The word "Maundy" comes from the Latin word "mandatum," meaning commandment, referring to Jesus' commandment to love one another as he has loved us (John 13:34).

The main liturgical celebration of Holy Thursday is the Mass of the Lord's Supper. This Mass is unique in several ways. Firstly, it includes the ritual of the washing of the feet, where the priest washes the feet of twelve people, symbolizing Jesus' act of humility and service to his disciples (John 13:1-17). This ritual reminds us of the importance of humility and service in the Christian life.

Secondly, during the Mass of the Lord's Supper, the Eucharist is consecrated as usual, but it is not followed by the usual procession and reservation of the Blessed Sacrament. Instead, the Blessed Sacrament is removed from the tabernacle, and the altar is stripped bare. This symbolizes the desolation of Christ's disciples after his arrest and the stripping of his garments before his crucifixion.

After the Mass, there is a procession of the Blessed Sacrament to the altar of repose, where it is reserved for Good Friday. This procession symbolizes Jesus' journey to the Garden of Gethsemane after the Last Supper, where he prayed before his arrest (Matthew 26:36-46).

Holy Thursday is a day of solemn reflection on the events of the Last Supper and the beginning of Jesus' Passion. It is a reminder of Jesus' love for us and his call to love one another. As we participate in the rituals of Holy Thursday, we are invited to deepen our commitment to following Jesus' example of humility, service, and love.

21

Holy Thursday

Holy Thursday, also known as Maundy Thursday, is a significant day in the liturgical calendar of the Catholic Church. It marks the beginning of the Easter Triduum, the three-day period leading up to Easter Sunday, which commemorates the Passion, Death, and Resurrection of Jesus Christ. Holy Thursday is particularly meaningful as it commemorates the Last Supper, where Jesus instituted the sacrament of the Eucharist and the priesthood.

1. **Institution of the Eucharist:** On Holy Thursday, we remember Jesus' Last Supper with his disciples, where he took bread, blessed it, broke it, and gave it to them, saying, "This is my body, which is given for you. Do this in remembrance of me" (Luke 22:19). This act established the Eucharist as a central sacrament of the Christian faith, where Catholics believe that the bread and wine become the body and blood of Christ through transubstantiation.

2. **Institution of the Priesthood:** During the Last Supper,

Jesus also instituted the priesthood. He washed the feet of his disciples, setting an example of humble service, and then instructed them to do the same for others. Jesus said, "If I, your Lord and Teacher, have washed your feet, you also ought to wash one another's feet" (John 13:14). This act symbolizes the call to service and selflessness that is central to the priesthood.

3. **The Agony in the Garden:** After the Last Supper, Jesus went to the Garden of Gethsemane to pray. He was deeply troubled and asked his disciples to stay awake and pray with him. Jesus prayed, "Father, if you are willing, remove this cup from me. Nevertheless, not my will, but yours, be done" (Luke 22:42). This moment reflects Jesus' human nature, as he faced the impending suffering and death that awaited him.

4. **TheBetrayalbyJudas:** HolyThursdayalsomarksthe betrayal of Jesus by Judas Iscariot. Judas, one of Jesus' disciples, agreed to betray him to the religious authorities for thirty pieces of silver. Judas' betrayal fulfilled the prophecy in the Old Testament, "Even my close friend in whom I trusted, who ate my bread, has lifted his heel against me" (Psalm 41:9).

5. **The Institution of the New Commandment:** During the Last Supper, Jesus gave his disciples a new commandment, saying, "A new commandment I give to you, that you love one another: just as I have loved you, you also are to love one another" (John 13:34). This commandment emphasizes the importance of love and unity among believers, reflecting the selfless love that Jesus demonstrated through his life and death.

6. **Preparation for the Crucifixion:** Holy Thursday sets the

stage for Good Friday, the day of Jesus' crucifixion. After the Last Supper, Jesus was arrested, tried, and ultimately sentenced to death on the cross. Holy Thursday reminds us of the sacrifice that Jesus made for our salvation and invites us to reflect on the depth of his love for us.

In conclusion, Holy Thursday is a solemn and sacred day in the Catholic Church. It reminds us of the profound events that took place during Jesus' final hours before his crucifixion. It is a time to reflect on the meaning of the Eucharist, the priesthood, and the call to love and serve one another as Jesus did. Holy Thursday invites us to enter into the mystery of Christ's passion and to deepen our commitment to living out his teachings in our daily lives.

22

Good Friday

Reflecting on the Crucifixion of Our Lord

On Good Friday, the Catholic Church commemorates the cruci- fixion and death of Jesus Christ, the Son of God. It is a solemn day of prayer, fasting, and reflection on the sacrifice that Jesus made for all humanity. This day is part of the Easter Triduum, which includes Holy Thursday, Good Friday, and Holy Saturday, leading up to the celebration of Easter Sunday.

The Significance of Good Friday

Good Friday holds immense significance in the Christian faith as it marks the day when Jesus willingly laid down His life for the redemption of mankind. According to Christian belief, Jesus, being fully divine and fully human, took on the sins of the world upon Himself and offered Himself as a perfect sacrifice to atone for humanity's sins. This act of selfless love and sacrifice is central to Christian theology and is seen as the ultimate expression of God's love for humanity.

Biblical Basis for Good Friday

The events of Good Friday are deeply rooted in biblical narratives, particularly in the Gospels. According to the Gospel accounts, Jesus was betrayed by Judas Iscariot, arrested by the Roman authorities, and subjected to a series of trials before the Jewish leaders and the Roman governor, Pontius Pilate. Despite being found innocent, Jesus was sentenced to death by crucifixion, a form of execution reserved for the most serious criminals.

The Gospel of Matthew (27:45-54) records the darkness that covered the land from noon until 3 p.m. while Jesus hung on the cross. In His final moments, Jesus cried out, "My God, my God, why have you forsaken me?" (Matthew 27:46), echoing the words of Psalm 22:1. This cry reflects the depth of Jesus' suffering and His identification with the human experience of feeling abandoned or forsaken.

The Agony of the Cross

The crucifixion itself was a brutal and agonizing form of execution. Jesus endured physical pain, humiliation, and mockery as He hung on the cross. Despite His suffering, Jesus demonstrated remarkable compassion and forgiveness, pray- ing for His enemies and promising paradise to the repentant thief who was crucified alongside Him (Luke 23:34, 43).

The Atoning Sacrifice

Central to Christian belief is the understanding that Jesus' death on the cross was not a tragic accident but a deliberate and necessary act of redemption. The Letter to the Hebrews describes Jesus as the high priest who offers Himself as a sacrifice to God, once for all, to take away the sins of the people (Hebrews 9:11-14).

The Meaning of the Cross

The cross, which was a symbol of shame and defeat, became the ultimate symbol of victory and salvation for Christians. St. Paul writes, "But far be it from me to boast except in the cross of our Lord Jesus Christ, by which the world has been crucified to me, and I to the world" (Galatians 6:14). The cross is a reminder of God's love and the lengths to which He was willing to go to reconcile humanity to Himself.

Observance of Good Friday

On Good Friday, Catholics and many other Christians observe the day with fasting, abstinence from meat, and solemn liturgical services. The liturgy typically includes the reading of the Passion narrative, veneration of the cross, and prayers of intercession for the Church and the world.

Conclusion

Good Friday is a day of profound significance for Christians worldwide. It is a day to reflect on the sacrifice of Jesus Christ and to ponder the depth of God's love for humanity. As we contemplate the crucifixion, may we be reminded of the power of God's redeeming love and the hope that it brings to all who believe.

23

Easter Vigil

The Easter Vigil is one of the most significant liturgical celebra- tions in the Catholic Church. It takes place on the evening of Holy Saturday, marking the culmination of the Triduum and the beginning of the Easter season. The Vigil is a profound and richly symbolic liturgy that reflects the paschal mystery of Christ's death and resurrection. It is a time of anticipation, joy, and hope as we await the resurrection of the Lord.

The Vigil is divided into four parts: The Service of Light, The Liturgy of the Word, The Liturgy of Baptism and Confirmation (or Renewal of Baptismal Promises), and the Liturgy of the Eucharist. Each part is filled with profound symbolism and meaning, drawing us deeper into the mystery of our faith.

1. The Service of Light:
The Easter Vigil begins in darkness, symbolizing the darkness of sin and death. A new fire is lit outside the church, symbolizing the light of Christ that dispels the darkness. This fire is used to light the Paschal Candle, which symbolizes Christ, the light of

the world. As the Paschal Candle is processed into the church, the darkness is gradually dispelled, symbolizing the light of Christ shining in the darkness of the world.

Biblical Example: "The light shines in the darkness, and the darkness has not overcome it." (John 1:5)

2. The Liturgy of the Word:

The Liturgy of the Word consists of a series of readings from the Old Testament that recount God's saving deeds throughout history, culminating in the resurrection of Christ. These readings are meant to show how God has always been at work in the world, leading His people from darkness to light.

The readings typically include the story of creation, the deliverance of the Israelites from slavery in Egypt, and prophecies foretelling the coming of the Messiah. The Liturgy of the Word concludes with the proclamation of the Easter Gospel, which announces the resurrection of Christ.

Biblical Example: "He is not here; he has risen, just as he said. Come and see the place where he lay." (Matthew 28:6)

3. The Liturgy of Baptism and Confirmation (or Renewal of Baptismal Promises):

The Easter Vigil is also a time when catechumens (those preparing for baptism) are initiated into the Church through the sacraments of baptism and confirmation. For those already baptized, it is a time to renew their baptismal promises and recommit themselves to their faith.

Baptism is a sacrament of initiation and purification, symbolizing the washing away of sin and the new life in Christ. Confirmation is a sacrament of strengthening, empowering the newly baptized with the gifts of the Holy Spirit.

Biblical Example: "For you were buried with Christ when you were baptized. And with him you were raised to new life because you trusted the mighty power of God, who raised Christ from the dead." (Colossians 2:12)

4. The Liturgy of the Eucharist:
The Easter Vigil concludes with the celebration of the Eucharist, where the faithful receive the body and blood of Christ. This sacrament is a source of nourishment and strength, enabling us to live out our faith in the world.

The Easter Vigil is a powerful and moving liturgy that reminds us of the central mystery of our faith: Christ has died, Christ is risen, Christ will come again. It is a time of great rejoicing as we celebrate the victory of Christ over sin and death, and look forward to the promise of eternal life.

In conclusion, the Easter Vigil is a profound liturgical celebration that invites us to journey from darkness to light, from death to life. It is a time to reflect on the paschal mystery of Christ's death and resurrection, and to renew our commitment to living out our faith in the world. As we celebrate the Easter Vigil, may we be filled with joy and hope, knowing that Christ has conquered sin and death, and has opened the gates of heaven for us.

25

Easter

Easter is the most important feast in the Christian liturgical calendar, celebrating the resurrection of Jesus Christ from the dead, as described in the New Testament. It is a time of great joy and hope for Christians around the world, as it represents the triumph of life over death and the promise of eternal life for all believers.

The Meaning of Easter

At its core, Easter is a celebration of the central mystery of the Christian faith: the resurrection of Jesus Christ. According to the Gospels, Jesus was crucified, died, and was buried, but on the third day, he rose again from the dead. This event is the foundation of the Christian faith, as it demonstrates Jesus' victory over sin and death and his ability to offer eternal life to all who believe in him.

The resurrection is not just a historical event; it is a theological reality that has profound implications for the lives of believers. It is a sign of God's power and love, showing that he has the power to conquer death and that he offers the gift of eternal life to all who believe in him. As St. Paul writes, "If Christ has not been raised, your faith is futile; you are still in your sins" (1 Corinthians 15:17).

The Easter Season

The Easter season begins on Easter Sunday and lasts for fifty days, culminating in the feast of Pentecost. During this time, Christians celebrate the resurrection of Jesus and reflect on its meaning for their lives. It is a time of joy and celebration, marked by special liturgies and traditions.

One of the key themes of the Easter season is the idea of new life. Just as Jesus rose from the dead, Christians believe that they too can experience new life through their faith in him. This is symbolized by the new life that emerges in nature during the springtime, as plants and flowers bloom and the earth is renewed.

Easter Traditions and Symbols

There are many traditions and symbols associated with Easter, each of which carries its own significance. One of the most common symbols is the Easter egg, which represents new life and the resurrection. The tradition of decorating eggs is thought to have originated in ancient times, when eggs were forbidden during Lent and were therefore saved and decorated as a special treat for Easter.

Another common tradition is the Easter bunny, which is said to bring eggs to children on Easter Sunday. While the origins of this tradition are unclear, it is thought to have its roots in pagan spring festivals that celebrated fertility and new life.

Biblical Examples

The resurrection of Jesus is described in all four Gospels, with each providing its own account of the event. In the Gospel of Matthew, Mary Magdalene and the other Mary go to Jesus' tomb and find it empty, with an angel telling them that Jesus has been raised from the dead (Matthew 28:1-10). In the Gospel of Mark, Mary Magdalene, Mary the mother of James, and Salome go to the tomb and find it empty, with a young man telling them that Jesus has been raised (Mark 16:1-8).

In the Gospel of Luke, the women go to the tomb and find it empty, with two men in dazzling clothes telling them that Jesus has been raised (Luke 24:1-12). In the Gospel of John, Mary Magdalene goes to the tomb and finds it empty, with Jesus appearing to her shortly thereafter (John 20:1-18).

These accounts of the resurrection serve as the basis for the Christian belief in the resurrection and provide the foundation for the Easter celebration. They are a reminder of the central message of Easter: that Jesus has conquered death and offers the hope of new life to all who believe in him.

26

Celebration of the Resurrection

The celebration of the Resurrection of Jesus Christ is the pinna- cle of the Christian faith and the most significant event in the liturgical calendar. It is the foundation of our hope as Christians and the source of our salvation. The Resurrection marks the victory of life over death, sin, and darkness. It is a celebration of new life, renewal, and the promise of eternal life with God.

The Resurrection is celebrated on Easter Sunday, which falls on the first Sunday after the full moon following the vernal equinox. This date varies each year but is always between March 22 and April 25. The Easter Vigil, held on Holy Saturday night, is the most solemn liturgy of the year and marks the beginning of the Easter celebration. It is a time of joyful anticipation as we await the Resurrection of the Lord.

The Easter Sunday Mass is a celebration of the Resurrection and is characterized by joyous hymns, readings from the Gospels recounting the Resurrection story, and the renewal of baptismal vows. The liturgical color for Easter is white, symbolizing purity and joy. The altar is adorned with flowers, and the church is filled with the fragrance of incense, symbolizing the prayers of the faithful rising to heaven.

The Resurrection is not just a historical event but a present reality in the life of every believer. St. Paul reminds us in his letter to the Romans, "If the Spirit of him who raised Jesus from the dead dwells in you, he who raised Christ Jesus from the dead will also give life to your mortal bodies through his Spirit who dwells in you" (Romans 8:11). This passage highlights the connection between the Resurrection of Jesus and the promise of new life for all who believe in him.

As we celebrate the Resurrection, we are reminded of the hope that we have in Christ. Just as Jesus conquered death and rose to new life, so too are we called to die to sin and rise to new life with him. This is expressed in the sacrament of baptism, where we are buried with Christ in his death and raised to new life with him (Romans 6:4).

The Resurrection also has profound implications for our daily lives. It reminds us that no matter what trials or tribulations we may face, we have the hope of eternal life with God. As St. Paul writes, "For this light momentary affliction is preparing for us an eternal weight of glory beyond all comparison" (2 Corinthians 4:17). This passage encourages us to persevere in faith, knowing that our present sufferings are nothing compared to the glory that awaits us in heaven.

In conclusion, the celebration of the Resurrection is a time of great joy and hope for Christians. It reminds us of the victory of life over death and the promise of eternal life with God. As we celebrate Easter, let us rejoice in the Resurrection of our Lord and Savior Jesus Christ and renew our commitment to living as his disciples, bearing witness to his love and mercy in the world.

27

The season of Easter

The Season of Easter is a sacred and joyous time in the liturgical calendar of the Catholic Church. It is a season of great significance, as it celebrates the central mystery of our faith: the Resurrection of Jesus Christ. Lasting for fifty days, from Easter Sunday until Pentecost, the Season of Easter is a period of profound rejoicing and reflection on the implications of Christ's victory over sin and death.

1. **Easter Sunday**: The Season of Easter begins with Easter Sunday, the most important feast day in the Christian calendar. On this day, we commemorate the resurrection of Jesus Christ from the dead, as narrated in the Gospels. The resurrection is the cornerstone of our faith, for as St. Paul writes, "if Christ has not been raised, your faith is futile; you are still in your sins" (1 Corinthians 15:17).
2. **Octave of Easter**: The eight days following Easter Sunday are known as the Octave of Easter, during which each day is considered a continuation of the feast of Easter. The Church's liturgy during this time is particularly rich in

joyful hymns and readings that proclaim the resurrection of Christ.

3. **Eastertide**: The entire Season of Easter, including the Octave of Easter, is often referred to as Eastertide. During this season, the Church's liturgical color is white, symbolizing joy and purity.

4. **Resurrection appearances**: Throughout the Season of Easter, the Gospels recount various appearances of the risen Christ to his disciples. These appearances serve as a confirmation of the reality of the resurrection and as a source of encouragement for believers. For example, in the Gospel of Luke, Jesus appears to his disciples on the road to Emmaus, revealing himself in the breaking of bread (Luke 24:13-35).

5. **The Great Commission**: One of the key themes of the Season of Easter is the mission given to the disciples by the risen Christ. Before ascending into heaven, Jesus instructs his disciples to go and make disciples of all nations, baptizing them in the name of the Father, and of the Son, and of the Holy Spirit (Matthew 28:19-20). This commissioning highlights the universal nature of the Christian faith and the call to share the good news of the resurrection with all people.

6. **Pentecost**: The Season of Easter concludes with the feast of Pentecost, which commemorates the outpouring of the Holy Spirit upon the disciples. This event marked the beginning of the Church's mission to proclaim the Gospel to the ends of the earth. Pentecost serves as a reminder of the ongoing presence and work of the Holy Spirit in the life of the Church and in the hearts of believers.

In summary, the Season of Easter is a time of great joy and celebration, as we rejoice in the victory of Christ over sin and death. It is a season that calls us to reflect on the profound implications of the resurrection for our lives and to renew our commitment to living as disciples of the risen Lord. As we journey through this season, may we be filled with the hope and joy that come from knowing that Christ is risen, alleluia!

28

Liturgical Readings and Prayers for Easter

As we delve into the liturgical readings and prayers for Easter, we are invited to explore the profound mystery and joy of Christ's resurrection. Easter, the greatest feast in the Christian calendar, celebrates the victory of life over death, light over darkness, and hope over despair. The readings and prayers during this season are carefully selected to reflect this central theme of resurrection and new life.

1. **Easter Vigil Readings**: The Easter Vigil is the most solemn celebration of the liturgical year. It begins in darkness, symbolizing the darkness of sin and death, but then a new fire is lit, symbolizing the light of Christ. The readings during the Easter Vigil recount the history of salvation, from the creation of the world to the resurrection of Jesus. They include the story of the Israelites' deliverance from slavery in Egypt (Exodus 14:15-15:1), which prefigures our liberation from sin through Christ's death and resurrection. The Easter Vigil readings also include the prophecy

74

of Ezekiel (Ezekiel 36:16-28), foretelling the restoration of Israel, which can be seen as a foreshadowing of the new life and new covenant we receive through Christ's resurrection.

2. **Resurrection Narratives**: Throughout the Easter season, the Gospels recount various appearances of the risen Christ to his disciples. These narratives not only testify to the reality of the resurrection but also reveal the transformative power of Christ's victory over death. One such example is the story of the disciples on the road to Emmaus (Luke 24:13-35), where Jesus appears to two disciples who are discouraged and confused after his death. Through his teaching and the breaking of bread, Jesus opens their eyes to recognize him, bringing them from despair to joy and faith.

3. **Pauline Epistles**: The letters of St. Paul during the Easter season often focus on the implications of Christ's resurrection for the Christian life. In his first letter to the Corinthians, Paul speaks of the resurrection as the foundation of our faith: "If Christ has not been raised, your faith is futile" (1 Corinthians 15:17). He also speaks of the transformative power of the resurrection, saying, "Therefore, if anyone is in Christ, the new creation has come: The old has gone, the new is here!" (2 Corinthians 5:17). These readings remind us that the resurrection is not just an event in the past but a reality that continues to transform our lives today.

4. **Prayers of Thanksgiving**: The prayers during the Easter season are filled with thanksgiving and praise for the gift of new life in Christ. The Easter Preface, which is prayed during the Eucharistic Prayer, captures this spirit

75

of gratitude: "For by your resurrection, you have given us new life, and by your ascension, you have opened the way to eternal life." These prayers remind us to give thanks to God for the gift of salvation and to live each day in the light of Christ's resurrection.

In conclusion, the liturgical readings and prayers for Easter invite us to enter more deeply into the mystery of Christ's resurrection and to allow its power to transform our lives. They remind us that the resurrection is not just a historical event but a present reality that gives us hope and joy. As we celebrate Easter, may we be filled with gratitude for the gift of new life in Christ and may we live each day in the light of his resurrection.

30

Ordinary Time II

In the liturgical calendar of the Roman Catholic Church, Ordinary Time is divided into two periods: Ordinary Time I and Ordinary Time II. These periods are not ordinary in the sense of being mundane or unimportant, but rather they are called "ordinary" because the weeks are numbered sequentially (e.g., the 1st Sunday of Ordinary Time, the 2nd Sunday of Ordinary Time, and so on) rather than being tied to a specific feast or season like Advent, Lent, or Easter.

Ordinary Time II begins after the Feast of the Baptism of the Lord and continues until the beginning of Lent, encompassing several weeks of the liturgical year. During this time, the focus is on the teachings and ministry of Jesus Christ, particularly his miracles, parables, and interactions with his disciples and the crowds.

The color green is used in liturgical decorations and vestments during Ordinary Time II, symbolizing hope, growth, and the ongoing life of the Church. Green reminds us of the need for continual spiritual growth and conversion in our lives as we follow Christ.

One of the key themes of Ordinary Time II is discipleship. Throughout the Gospels, Jesus calls people to follow him and become his disciples. For example, in Mark 1:17, Jesus says to Simon and Andrew, "Come, follow me, and I will make you fishers of men." This call to discipleship is not just for the apostles but for all believers. It challenges us to live as authentic followers of Christ, imitating his example of love, mercy, and service.

During Ordinary Time II, the readings from the Gospels often highlight the teachings and parables of Jesus. These stories offer us valuable lessons for our own lives and faith journeys. For example, the parable of the Good Samaritan (Luke 10:25-37) challenges us to show compassion and mercy to all people, even those who are different from us or whom we may consider enemies.

Another important aspect of Ordinary Time II is the focus on the mission of the Church. Just as Jesus sent out his disciples to preach the Gospel and heal the sick (Matthew 10:5-15), so too are we called to be missionaries of the Good News in our own time and place. This mission involves not only proclaiming the Gospel with our words but also living it out in our actions and relationships.

Overall, Ordinary Time II is a time for us to deepen our relation- ship with Christ, grow in our understanding of his teachings, and live out our faith more fully in the world. It is a time of hope and renewal as we journey together as disciples of Jesus Christ.

31

Liturgical Readings and Prayers for Ordinary Time II

In Ordinary Time II, the liturgical readings and prayers guide the faithful through a period of growth and discipleship in their Christian journey. This season, marked by green vestments, is a time of reflection on the teachings and miracles of Jesus, encouraging believers to deepen their faith and commitment to God's kingdom.

1. **Weekdays in Ordinary Time II:** During the weekdays of Ordinary Time II, the readings from the Old Testament, Psalms, New Testament, and Gospel passages provide a rich tapestry of God's revelation and guidance for His people. These readings offer a continuous narrative of salvation history, highlighting the faithfulness of God and the call to respond in faith and obedience. For example, in the Old Testament, the story of Abraham's faithfulness and willingness to sacrifice his son Isaac (Genesis 22:1-19) serves as a model of trust in God's providence. This narrative parallels the ultimate sacrifice of Jesus, foreshadowing the redemptive work of Christ on the

cross.

The Psalms, often referred to as the prayer book of the Bible, offer words of praise, lament, and thanksgiving that resonate with the human experience. For instance, Psalm 23, a beloved passage, speaks of God's care and provision, portraying Him as a shepherd guiding His flock. This imagery reflects the intimate relationship between God and His people, emphasizing His constant presence and protection.

In the New Testament readings, the teachings of Jesus and the apostles provide insights into the nature of discipleship and the kingdom of God. For example, the Sermon on the Mount (Matthew 5-7) contains foundational teachings of Jesus, including the Beatitudes, which outline the characteristics of true discipleship. These teachings challenge believers to embody virtues such as humility, mercy, and peacemaking, reflecting the values of God's kingdom.

The Gospel passages in Ordinary Time II feature various miracles and parables of Jesus, illustrating His power and authority as the Son of God. For instance, the multiplication of the loaves and fishes (John 6:1-15) demonstrates Jesus' ability to provide for the physical and spiritual needs of His followers. This miracle points to the Eucharist as a source of nourishment and sustenance for believers, highlighting the importance of the sacraments in the life of the Church.

2. Sundays in Ordinary Time II: The Sundays in Ordinary Time II focus on the public ministry of Jesus, highlighting His teachings, miracles, and interactions with various individuals.

Each Sunday offers a unique theme that invites believers to reflect on different aspects of discipleship and faith.

- **First Sunday**: The readings often focus on the call of disciple- ship and the response of individuals to Jesus' invitation. For example, the calling of the first disciples (Matthew 4:18-22) illustrates the immediacy and radical nature of following Jesus. This passage challenges believers to prioritize their relationship with Christ above all else, leaving behind their old way of life to embrace a new identity as His followers.

- **Second Sunday**: Themes of healing and restoration are common, highlighting Jesus' compassion and power to heal physical, emotional, and spiritual ailments. For instance, the healing of the leper (Mark 1:40-45) demonstrates Jesus' will- ingness to reach out to the marginalized and outcast, offering them hope and restoration. This passage reminds believers of the importance of reaching out to those in need and extending God's love and mercy to all.

- **Third Sunday**: The theme of repentance and conversion is often emphasized, calling believers to turn away from sin and embrace a life of holiness. For example, the parable of the prodigal son (Luke 15:11-32) illustrates the Father's unconditional love and forgiveness, inviting sinners to return to Him with contrite hearts. This parable serves as a powerful reminder of God's mercy and the need for continual conversion in the Christian life.

- **Fourth Sunday**: The readings focus on the teachings of Jesus, emphasizing the importance of faith and trust in God's providence. For example, the parable of the mustard seed (Mark 4:30-32) illustrates the growth of God's kingdom from humble beginnings to a flourishing reality. This parable encourages believers to have faith in the transformative power of God's word and the small acts of faithfulness that contribute to the growth of His kingdom.

- **Fifth Sunday**: Themes of discipleship and service are often highlighted, challenging believers to live out their faith in concrete ways. For example, the call to service (Matthew 25:31- 46) reminds believers that their faith should be reflected in acts of charity and compassion towards others. This passage emphasizes the importance of loving one's neighbor as oneself, embodying the teachings of Jesus in everyday life.

Overall, the liturgical readings and prayers for Ordinary Time II invite believers to deepen their relationship with God, grow in faith and discipleship, and bear witness to the kingdom of God in the world. Through these readings, believers are called to live out their faith authentically, following the example of Christ and striving for holiness in their daily lives.

33

Solemnities, feasts, and memorials

Solemnities, feasts, and memorials are integral parts of the liturgical calendar of the Catholic Church, each with its own significance and purpose in the life of the faithful. These celebrations are not merely dates on a calendar but are opportunities for Catholics to deepen their faith and grow closer to God through the commemoration of key events, persons, and teachings of the Catholic tradition.

Solemnities are the highest-ranking celebrations in the liturgi- cal calendar. They mark major events in the life of Jesus Christ, the Blessed Virgin Mary, and the saints, as well as key teach- ings of the Catholic Church. Examples of solemnities include Christmas, Easter, Pentecost, the Immaculate Conception, and the Assumption of Mary. These celebrations are characterized by special liturgical rites, such as the Gloria and the Creed, and often involve additional readings and prayers that highlight the significance of the event or person being honored.

Feasts are celebrations of lesser rank than solemnities but

are still important occasions in the liturgical year. Feasts commemorate events in the life of Jesus, Mary, and the saints, as well as significant moments in the history of the Church. Examples of feasts include the Epiphany, the Baptism of the Lord, the Transfiguration, and the Feast of the Holy Family. Like solemnities, feasts are marked by special liturgical rites and readings that reflect the theme of the celebration.

Memorials are the lowest-ranking celebrations in the liturgical calendar but are still valuable opportunities for the faithful to remember and honor the saints and martyrs of the Church. Memorials are divided into three categories: obligatory memo- rials, which must be celebrated; optional memorials, which may be celebrated; and memorials of saints added to the General Roman Calendar after 1969, which are celebrated by those who have a particular devotion to the saint. Memorials are typically commemorated with a simple Mass, including the opening prayer, a reading or readings, and a prayer over the gifts.

In summary, solemnities, feasts, and memorials are important elements of the liturgical calendar that help Catholics to re- member and celebrate key events, persons, and teachings of the Catholic faith. These celebrations are not only opportunities for worship and prayer but also serve to deepen the faith of the faithful and strengthen their connection to the larger Catholic community. As the Catechism of the Catholic Church teaches, the liturgical year is "a year of grace, provided that [we] seek the light of the Holy Spirit in [the Church's] liturgy" (CCC 1095). By participating fully in the solemnities, feasts, and memorials of the Church, Catholics can grow in their understanding of the faith and experience the richness of God's love and mercy in their lives.

34

List of Solemnities, Feasts, and Memorials in the Liturgical Calendar

In the Roman Catholic liturgical calendar, the Church celebrates various solemnities, feasts, and memorials throughout the year. These liturgical celebrations help us to remember and honor the life, death, and resurrection of Jesus Christ, as well as the lives of the saints and martyrs who have gone before us in faith.

1. **Solemnities**: Solemnities are the highest ranking liturgical celebrations in the Church's calendar. They commemorate the most important events in the life of Christ and the Blessed Virgin Mary. Examples of solemnities include Christmas (the birth of Jesus), Easter (the resurrection of Jesus), and the Feast of the Assumption (the bodily assumption of Mary into heaven).

   - **Example**: The Feast of the Assumption is a solemnity that celebrates the belief that Mary, the mother of Jesus, was assumed body and soul into heaven at the end of her earthly life. This belief is not explicitly stated in the Bible, but it is based on the Catholic Church's tradition and the belief in Mary's special role in salvation history.

2. **Feasts**: Feasts are liturgical celebrations that honor the life and ministry of Jesus Christ, the Blessed Virgin Mary, and the saints. Feasts are ranked below solemnities but are still important occasions for prayer and worship. Examples of feasts include the Feast of the Holy Family, the Feast of the Immaculate Conception, and the Feast of Corpus Christi.

- **Example**: The Feast of Corpus Christi is a feast that celebrates the real presence of Jesus Christ in the Eucharist. This feast is based on the words of Jesus at the Last Supper, where he said, "This is my body, which is given for you" (Luke 22:19).

3. **Memorials**: Memorials are liturgical celebrations that honor the saints and martyrs of the Church. Memorials are divided into two categories: obligatory memorials and optional memo- rials. Obligatory memorials are commemorated throughout the universal Church, while optional memorials are celebrated only in certain regions or communities.

- **Example**: The Memorial of Saint Francis of Assisi is an optional memorial that honors the life and example of Saint Francis, the founder of the Franciscan Order. Saint Francis is known for his love of nature and his devotion to poverty and simplicity, as exemplified in his famous prayer, "Lord, make me an instrument of your peace".

Overall, the celebration of solemnities, feasts, and memorials in the liturgical calendar helps to enrich our spiritual lives and deepen our understanding of the mysteries of our faith. By participating in these liturgical celebrations, we are reminded of God's love for us and the communion of saints that surrounds us, encouraging us to live lives of holiness and virtue.

35

Liturgical Readings and Prayers for solemnities, feasts and memorials

In the liturgical life of the Catholic Church, solemnities, feasts, and memorials hold a special place. These liturgical celebra- tions allow us to delve deeper into the mysteries of our faith and to commemorate the lives of the saints who have gone before us. Each of these celebrations has its own unique readings and prayers, carefully selected to reflect the theme and significance of the occasion. Let us explore the liturgical readings and prayers for solemnities, feasts, and memorials, guided by the Word of God and the wisdom of the Church.

Solemnities

Solemnities are the highest-ranking liturgical celebrations in the Church's calendar. They mark important events in the life of Christ or significant aspects of the Church's teachings. The readings and prayers for solemnities are rich in theological depth and often highlight the central mysteries of our faith.

For example, the solemnity of the Most Holy Trinity focuses on the mystery of God as Father, Son, and Holy Spirit. The readings for this solemnity often include passages that speak to the nature of God, such as the Great Commission in Matthew 28:19-20, where Jesus instructs his disciples to baptize in the name of the Father, and of the Son, and of the Holy Spirit.

Feasts

Feasts are celebrations of lesser rank than solemnities but still hold great significance in the liturgical calendar. They commemorate events in the life of Christ, the Blessed Virgin Mary, or the saints. The readings and prayers for feasts are chosen to reflect the particular event or person being honored. For example, the feast of the Assumption of the Blessed Virgin Mary celebrates Mary's being taken up into heaven, body and soul, at the end of her earthly life. The readings for this feast often include the passage from the Book of Revelation (Revelation 12:1-6), which describes a woman clothed with the sun, with the moon under her feet, and on her head a crown of twelve stars, symbolizing Mary's role as Queen of Heaven.

Memorials

Memorials are the lowest-ranking celebrations in the Church's calendar but are still important opportunities to remember and honor the saints. The readings and prayers for memorials are chosen to reflect the life and virtues of the saint being commemorated.

For example, the memorial of St. Francis of Assisi might include readings that highlight his love for poverty and his care for creation, such as the Beatitudes (Matthew 5:3-12), which speak to the virtues of humility, meekness, and peacemaking tbat Francis exemplified in his life.

In conclusion, the liturgical readings and prayers for solemnities, feasts, and memorials are carefully chosen to deepen our understanding of the mysteries of our faith and to inspire us to follow the example of Christ and the saints. They remind us of the great cloud of witnesses that surrounds us (Hebrews 12:1) and encourage us to live lives of holiness and virtue. May we always be attentive to the Word of God proclaimed in these celebrations and strive to imitate the faith and devotion of those who have gone before us.

III

Daily mass readings

In Part II of the Roman Catholic Daily and Sunday Missal 2024, we delve into the heart of the daily Mass readings, where the Word of God is proclaimed and reflected upon by the faithful. Each day offers a unique opportunity to encounter the living Word of God and be nourished by it.

36

Weekdays in Ordinary Time

In the liturgical calendar of the Catholic Church, Ordinary Time is the period between the seasons of Christmas and Lent, and then again between Pentecost and Advent. It is called "ordinary" not because it is mundane or common, but because the weeks are numbered in sequence (from the Latin word "ordinalis," meaning numbered). This time is a reminder of the life and teachings of Jesus Christ and a call to live out our faith in our daily lives.

During Weekdays in Ordinary Time, the readings at Mass focus on various aspects of the Christian life, drawing from both the Old and New Testaments to provide guidance, encouragement, and instruction for believers. These readings are carefully selected to complement the themes of the liturgical season and to offer spiritual nourishment for the faithful.

Monday to Saturday Readings

Each weekday during Ordinary Time has its own set of readings, including a reading from the Old Testament, a Responsorial Psalm, a reading from the New Testament (usually from one of the epistles), and a Gospel reading. These readings are chosen to provide a coherent message for each day and to help the faithful deepen their understanding of Scripture and its relevance to their lives.

Reflections and Prayers for Weekday Readings

The readings for Weekdays in Ordinary Time offer a rich source of reflection and prayer for Catholics. They provide an opportunity to meditate on the Word of God and to apply its teachings to one's life. For example, a reading from the Book of Proverbs might offer wisdom for making good decisions, while a passage from one of the epistles might encourage believers to persevere in faith.

Biblical Examples

One biblical example of the importance of regular reading and reflection on Scripture is found in the book of Acts. In Acts 17:11, we read about the Berean Jews who "received the message with great eagerness and examined the Scriptures every day to see if what Paul said was true." This example reminds us of the value of daily engagement with the Word of God.

Another example is found in Psalm 1, which describes the blessedness of the one who meditates on God's law day and night. The psalmist compares such a person to a tree planted by streams of water, which yields its fruit in season and whose leaf does not wither (Psalm 1:3). This imagery highlights the nourishing and life-giving nature of regular reflection on Scripture.

Conclusion

Weekdays in Ordinary Time provide a valuable opportunity for Catholics to deepen their relationship with God through the reading and reflection on Scripture. By engaging with the daily Mass readings, believers can grow in their understanding of the Christian faith and its relevance to their daily lives.

37

Monday to Saturday Readings

In the liturgical calendar of the Roman Catholic Church, the readings for Mass on weekdays, from Monday to Saturday, are carefully selected to complement the themes of the liturgical season or to commemorate specific saints or events. These daily readings serve as a spiritual nourishment for the faithful, guiding them in their daily lives and deepening their under- standing of the faith. Let us delve into the significance of these readings and their relevance in our lives as Catholics.

Monday Readings:
Mondays in the liturgical calendar often focus on themes of renewal and beginnings. The readings may encourage us to start our week with a fresh perspective, renewing our commitment to live according to God's will. For example, in the Gospel of Luke (6:6-11), Jesus heals a man with a withered hand on the Sabbath, highlighting the importance of doing good and showing compassion, even on the first day of the week.

Tuesday Readings:

Tuesdays often emphasize the teachings of Jesus and the importance of discipleship. The readings may challenge us to deepen our understanding of the Gospel and to live out our faith more fully. In the Gospel of Mark (10:28-31), Jesus speaks about the rewards of discipleship, reassuring his followers that their sacrifices for the sake of the Gospel will not go unnoticed by God.

Wednesday Readings:
Wednesdays often focus on the call to conversion and repentance. The readings may remind us of the need to continually turn away from sin and to seek God's forgiveness. In the Gospel of Luke (11:42-46), Jesus rebukes the Pharisees for their hypocrisy, urging them to repent and change their ways.

Thursday Readings:
Thursdays often highlight the Eucharist and the importance of the Mass. The readings may deepen our appreciation for the sacrament of the Eucharist and its significance in our lives. In the Gospel of John (6:44-51), Jesus speaks about himself as the bread of life, emphasizing the spiritual nourishment that he provides through the Eucharist.

Friday Readings:
Fridays often focus on the passion and death of Jesus Christ. The readings may invite us to reflect on the sacrifice of Christ and to unite our sufferings with his. In the Gospel of John (19:25- 27), Jesus entrusts his mother Mary to the care of the beloved disciple, demonstrating his love and concern for us even in his final moments.

Saturday Readings:

Saturdays often commemorate the Blessed Virgin Mary and the saints. The readings may inspire us to emulate the faithfulness and devotion of the saints in our own lives. In the Gospel of Luke (1:39-56), we read about the Visitation, where Mary visits her cousin Elizabeth and magnifies the Lord for the great things he has done for her, setting an example of humility and faithfulness for all believers.

In conclusion, the weekday readings in the Roman Catholic liturgical calendar are rich in meaning and significance, offering us guidance and inspiration for our daily lives as Catholics. They remind us of the teachings of Jesus, the importance of discipleship, the need for conversion and repentance, the significance of the Eucharist, and the example of the saints. May we always be attentive to these readings and allow them to shape our lives according to God's will.

38

Reflections and Prayers for Weekday Readings

In the ordinary rhythm of the Church's liturgical life, weekdays offer us a unique opportunity for deeper reflection and spiritual growth. While Sundays are reserved for the celebration of the Lord's Resurrection, weekdays provide us with a chance to delve into the richness of Scripture and apply its teachings to our daily lives.

Each weekday, the Church presents us with specific readings — often from the Old Testament, the Psalms, and the New Testament—carefully selected to complement one another and convey a particular message. These readings are not random but are part of a carefully crafted plan that unfolds throughout the liturgical year, guiding us through the life of Christ and the teachings of the apostles.

Let us turn to the Bible for guidance on how we can reflect on and pray with the weekday readings:

1. **Old Testament Readings**: The Old Testament readings often provide a historical context or prophetic insight into God's plan for His people. For example, the story of Abraham's faithfulness in offering his son Isaac (Genesis 22:1-18) can remind us of the importance of trust and obedience in our relationship with God. We can reflect on how we can deepen our trust in God's providence and strive to be obedient to His will in our lives.

2. **Responsorial Psalm**: The Responsorial Psalm is a response to the first reading, offering praise, thanksgiving, or a plea for help. For example, Psalm 23, often read on weekdays, reminds us of God's loving care and protection, even in the midst of challenges. We can pray this psalm, asking God to be our shepherd and guide us in the paths of righteousness.

3. **New Testament Readings**: The New Testament readings, especially from the letters of St. Paul and other apostolic writings, provide practical advice and encouragement for living the Christian life. For example, Paul's exhortation to "rejoice always, pray without ceasing, give thanks in all circumstances" (1 Thessalonians 5:16-18) can inspire us to cultivate a spirit of gratitude and prayerfulness in our daily lives.

4. **Gospel Reading**: The Gospel reading is the highlight of the weekday liturgy, offering us direct teachings of Jesus or accounts of His ministry. For example, the parable of the Good Samaritan (Luke 10:25-37) challenges us to love our neighbors, even those who are different from us. We can reflect on how we can show compassion and mercy to others, following the example of Christ.

In reflecting on these readings, we are called to pray for the grace to understand God's Word more deeply and to apply it to our lives. We can ask God to open our hearts to His message and to give us the strength to live according to His will.

Let us also remember that the weekday readings are not just for our personal edification but are meant to be shared with others. We can discuss the readings with our families, friends, or fellow parishioners, allowing God's Word to inspire and guide us collectively.

As we delve into the weekday readings, let us remember the words of St. Paul: "All Scripture is inspired by God and is useful for teaching, for reproof, for correction, and for training in righteousness, so that everyone who belongs to God may be proficient, equipped for every good work" (2 Timothy 3:16-17). May the weekday readings nourish our souls and equip us to live as faithful disciples of Christ.

40

Sunday in Ordinary Time

Sunday in Ordinary Time is a pivotal day in the liturgical calendar of the Catholic Church. It is a day of great significance, marked by the celebration of the Eucharist and the gathering of the faithful to worship and give thanks to God. In this reflection, we will explore the richness and meaning of Sunday in Ordinary Time, drawing from the teachings of the Church and the wisdom of the Scriptures.

41

Sunday Readings

On Sundays, the Catholic Church gathers to celebrate the Eucharist, the source and summit of our faith. The Sunday liturgy is structured around the readings from the Bible, which are carefully selected to guide us through the liturgical year and deepen our understanding of God's plan of salvation. These readings are not chosen randomly; they are part of a carefully crafted cycle known as the Lectionary, which ensures that the faithful hear a wide range of Scripture passages over a three- year period.

1. **First Reading (Old Testament):** The first reading usually comes from the Old Testament and is chosen to corre-spondthematicallywiththeGospelreading. Ithelps us to understand the continuity between the Old and New Testaments and how God's plan of salvation unfolds throughout history. For example, during Advent, we hear readings from the prophets that anticipate the coming of the Messiah, such as Isaiah's prophecies about the virgin birth (Isaiah 7:14) and the shoot from the stump of Jesse

(Isaiah 11:1-10).

2. **Responsorial Psalm**: The Responsorial Psalm is a response to the first reading, often emphasizing its theme or providing a prayerful reflection. The psalms are songs of praise, lament, thanksgiving, and supplication that express the full range of human emotions and experiences. They remind us of the importance of prayer and praise in our relationship with God. For example, Psalm 23 is often chosen for its comforting imagery of God as a shepherd who guides and protects his flock.

3. Second Reading (New Testament): The second reading usually comes from one of the epistles (letters) in the New Testament, written by St. Paul or other early Christian leaders. These readings offer practical guidance for Christian living and often emphasize the importance of faith, love, and good works. For example, in his letter to the Corinthians, St. Paul speaks about the importance of unity in the Body of Christ (1 Corinthians 12:12-30).

4. **GospelReading**: TheGospelreadingisthehighpointof the Liturgy of the Word and is proclaimed by a priest or deacon. It is always taken from one of the four Gospels (Matthew, Mark, Luke, or John) and is the most important reading of the Mass. The Gospel recounts the words and deeds of Jesus Christ, providing us with direct insights into his teachings and actions. For example, in the Gospel of John, Jesus performs his first miracle at the wedding feast in Cana (John 2:1-11), revealing his divine power and his concern for our everyday needs.

5. **Homily**: After the Gospel reading, the priest or deacon delivers a homily, which is a reflection on the readings and their significance for our lives. The homily is meant to

help us understand the Word of God more deeply and apply it to our daily lives. It is an opportunity for the priest to offer spiritual guidance and encouragement to the faithful. For example, the priest may reflect on the theme of mercy in the readings and challenge us to show mercy to others as God has shown mercy to us (Luke 6:36).

6. **Prayers of the Faithful**: The Liturgy of the Word concludes with the Prayers of the Faithful, also known as the Universal Prayer or the Prayer of the Faithful. In these prayers, we intercede for the needs of the Church and the world, expressing our concerns and hopes to God. We pray for the Church, for those in authority, for the sick and suffering, for the faithful departed, and for our own intentions. These prayers remind us of our responsibility to care for one another and to bring our needs before God in prayer.

42

Reflections and Prayers for Sunday Readings

Each Sunday, Catholics gather to celebrate the Eucharist, the central act of Christian worship. The Sunday liturgy is structured around the readings from Scripture, which are carefully chosen to guide and inspire the faithful. These readings, along with the prayers and reflections that accompany them, provide a rich source of spiritual nourishment and guidance for living out our faith in the world.

1. **First Reading**: The first reading, usually taken from the Old Testament, sets the stage for the Gospel reading by foreshadowing the coming of Christ or highlighting an important theme. For example, in Isaiah 55:1-3, we hear an invitation to come to the Lord and receive the blessings of salvation, a theme that is echoed in the Gospel reading.
2. **Responsorial Psalm**: The Responsorial Psalm is a response to the first reading, often focusing on themes of praise, thanksgiving, and trust in God's providence. It is

a reminder of God's faithfulness throughout history and a call to respond with faith and gratitude. For instance, in Psalm 63:2, we hear the psalmist's longing for God's presence and his acknowledgment that God's love is better than life itself.

3. **Second Reading**: The second reading, usually from the New Testament letters, provides practical instruction for Christian living. It often highlights the implications of the Gospel message for our daily lives. For example, in Romans 8:28-30, St. Paul assures us that God works all things for the good of those who love him, encouraging us to trust in God's providence.

4. **Gospel Reading**: The Gospel reading is the high point of the Liturgy of the Word, as it contains the words and actions of Jesus himself. The Gospel readings are carefully chosen to present a coherent message over the course of the liturgical year, leading us through the life, teachings, and saving work of Jesus. For example, in Mark 10:46-52, we hear the story of Bartimaeus, a blind man who receives his sight after calling out to Jesus in faith, reminding us of the power of faith and Jesus' compassion for the marginalized.

5. **Homily**: The homily is a commentary on the Scripture readings, intended to help the faithful understand and apply God's word to their lives. It is an opportunity for the priest or deacon to explain the meaning of the readings and to offer practical insights for living out the Gospel message. The homily should be rooted in the teachings of the Church and should seek to inspire and challenge the faithful to grow in their faith and discipleship.

6. **Prayers of the Faithful**: Also known as the Universal

Prayer or the Prayer of the Faithful, this is a series of petitions offered on behalf of the Church and the world. The prayers usually include intentions for the Church, the civil authorities, those in need, and the local community. They are a reminder of our responsibility to pray for the needs of others and to be mindful of the larger community of faith.

In conclusion, the Sunday readings, along with the prayers and reflections that accompany them, are a vital source of spiritual nourishment for Catholics. They offer us a roadmap for living out our faith in the world, guiding us in our relationship with God and with one another. As we reflect on the Sunday readings and pray for God's guidance and grace, may we be inspired to live out the Gospel message in our daily lives, bearing witness to the love and mercy of Christ in all that we do.

44

Special Liturgical Days

In the liturgical calendar of the Catholic Church, certain days hold a special significance, inviting us to delve deeper into the mysteries of our faith and to reflect on key events in the life of Christ and the Church. These special days, including solemnities, feasts, and memorials, are not merely dates on a calendar but are moments of grace and opportunity for spiritual growth and renewal. Let us explore the richness of these special liturgical days and their profound meaning for our Christian journey.

1. Solemnities: Solemnities are the highest-ranking liturgical celebrations in the Church's calendar. They commemorate the most important mysteries of the Christian faith, such as the Nativity of Christ, the Resurrection, and the Assumption of Mary. Solemnitiesinviteustoentermoredeeplyinto these central mysteries of our salvation and to ponder their significance in our lives.

Example: The Feast of the Immaculate Conception (December 8th) celebrates the belief that Mary, the mother of Jesus, was conceived without original sin. This solemnity highlights Mary's unique role in salvation history and reminds us of her perfect obedience to God's will.

2. **Feasts**: Feasts are celebrations of saints, angels, or other events that hold a special place in the life of the Church. They allow us to honor those who have gone before us in faith and to seek their intercession and example in our own lives. Feasts also commemorate important moments in the life of Christ, such as the Baptism of the Lord or the Transfiguration.

Example: The Feast of St. Francis of Assisi (October 4th) commemorates the life of St. Francis, who embraced a life of poverty and simplicity in imitation of Christ. This feast encourages us to live out the Gospel values of humility, charity, and care for creation.

3. **Memorials**: Memorials are celebrations of saints or events that are of lesser importance than feasts but still hold significance for the Church. They remind us of the holiness and heroic virtue of the saints and encourage us to follow their example in our own lives.

Example: The Memorial of St. Teresa of Calcutta (September 5th) honors the life and work of Mother Teresa, who dedicated her life to serving the poorest of the poor. This memorial challenges us to reach out in love and compassion to those in need around us.

Each of these special liturgical days offers us a unique opportu- nity to deepen our relationship with God and to grow in holiness. By participating in the celebrations of the Church's calendar, we unite ourselves with the whole Body of Christ and open ourselves to the transforming power of God's grace.

As St. Paul reminds us in Colossians 3:16, "Let the word of Christ dwell in you richly, teaching and admonishing one another in all wisdom, singing psalms and hymns and spiritual songs, with thankfulness in your hearts to God." May we approach these special liturgical days with hearts full of gratitude and praise, ready to receive the abundant blessings that God wishes to bestow upon us.

45

Reading and prayers for special occasions

As we journey through the liturgical year, there are special occasions that call for readings and prayers that reflect the significance of these moments in the life of the Church and of individual believers. These occasions provide opportunities for us to deepen our faith, express our gratitude, seek forgiveness, and ask for God's guidance and protection. Let us explore some of these special occasions and the readings and prayers associated with them.

1. **Feast of the Holy Family**: Celebrated on the Sunday after Christmas, this feast honors the Holy Family of Jesus, Mary, and Joseph. It reminds us of the importance of family life and the virtues of love, obedience, and humility. The readings for this feast often focus on the Holy Family as a model for Christian families (Colossians 3:12-21).

2. **Feast of the Baptism of the Lord**: This feast marks the end of the Christmas season and the beginning of Jesus' public ministry. The readings highlight the importance

of baptism and the mission of Jesus as the beloved Son of God (Mark 1:7-11).

3. **Ash Wednesday**: Ash Wednesday marks the beginning of Lent, a season of fasting, prayer, and repentance. The readings for Ash Wednesday call us to repentance and conversion, reminding us of our mortality and the need to turn away from sin (Joel 2:12-18).

4. **Palm Sunday**: Palm Sunday commemorates Jesus' triumphal entry into Jerusalem. The readings for this day include the account of Jesus' entry into Jerusalem and the Passion narrative, reminding us of the events leading up to Jesus' crucifixion (Matthew 21:1-11, Mark 14:1-15:47).

5. **Holy Thursday**: Holy Thursday marks the beginning of the Easter Triduum and commemorates the Last Supper, where Jesus instituted the Eucharist and washed the feet of his disciples. The readings for Holy Thursday focus on the institution of the Eucharist and the call to love and serve one another (John 13:1-15).

6. **Good Friday**: Good Friday commemorates the crucifixion of Jesus. The readings for Good Friday include the Passion narrative and reflections on the suffering and death of Jesus for our salvation (John 18:1-19:42).

7. **HolySaturday**: HolySaturdayisadayofquietreflection and anticipation as we await the celebration of Jesus' resurrection. The readings for Holy Saturday often include the Easter Vigil readings, which recount salvation history and culminate in the celebration of Jesus' resurrection (Romans 6:3-11).

8. **All Saints' Day**: All Saints' Day honors all the saints, known and unknown, who have lived lives of holiness and are now in the presence of God. The readings for All Saints'

Day often focus on the call to holiness and the promise of eternal life (Revelation 7:9-17).

9. **All Souls' Day**: All Souls' Day is a day to remember and pray for all the faithful departed. The readings for All Souls' Day often focus on the hope of resurrection and the promise of eternal life (1 Thessalonians 4:13-18).

10. **Feast of Christ the King**: The Feast of Christ the King is celebrated on the last Sunday of the liturgical year and honors Jesus as the King of the Universe. The readings for this feast often focus on the kingship of Christ and the call to acknowledge him as our Lord and Savior (Colossians 1:15-20).

These special occasions remind us of the central mysteries of our faith and invite us to deepen our relationship with God. Through the readings and prayers associated with these occasions, we are called to reflect on the meaning of these mysteries in our own lives and to respond with faith, love, and devotion.

46

Reflection on special liturgical days

Special liturgical days within the Catholic calendar hold profound significance, offering unique opportunities for reflection and spiritual growth. These days are marked by their associ- ation with key events in the life of Jesus Christ or important figures in Christian history. Each special day invites us to delve deeper into our faith, drawing inspiration from the examples set before us and finding renewed strength in our journey of discipleship.

1. **Feast of the Immaculate Conception**: Celebrated on Decem- ber 8th, this feast commemorates the belief that the Blessed Virgin Mary was preserved from original sin from the moment of her conception. This feast reminds us of Mary's unique role in salvation history and her complete devotion to God. The Immaculate Conception serves as a prelude to the birth of Jesus, highlighting Mary's purity and her cooperation with God's plan for humanity's redemption.

    Biblical Example: In Luke 1:28, the angel Gabriel greets Mary by saying, "Hail, full of grace, the Lord is with you."

This greeting is seen as an affirmation of Mary's immaculate conception, as she is described as "full of grace" from the beginning of her existence.

2. All Saints' Day: Celebrated on November 1st, All Saints' Day honors all the saints, known and unknown, who have attained heaven. This day emphasizes the communion of saints, the belief that all believers, living and dead, are united in Christ. It reminds us of the universal call to holiness and the diverse ways in which individuals have lived out their faith throughout history.
Biblical Example: Revelation 7:9-10 describes a great multitude from every nation, tribe, people, and language standing before the throne and before the Lamb, wearing white robes and holding palm branches, signifying the saints who have been glorified in heaven.

3. Feast of the Ascension: Celebrated on the 40th day of Easter, the Feast of the Ascension commemorates Jesus' ascension into heaven. This event marks the culmination of Jesus' earthly ministry and his return to the Father's side. The Ascension reminds us of Jesus' promise to prepare a place for us and his commission to spread the Gospel to all nations.
Biblical Example: Acts 1:9-11 describes the Ascension, where Jesus is taken up into heaven in the presence of his disciples, with a promise that he will return in the same way he ascended.

4. Solemnity of the Most Holy Trinity: Celebrated on the Sunday after Pentecost, this solemnity honors the three persons of the Trinity: the Father, the Son, and the Holy Spirit. It is a reminder of the central mystery of the Christian faith and invites us to contemplate the nature of God's unity and love.

Biblical Example: Matthew 28:19 records Jesus' instruction to his disciples to baptize in the name of the Father, and of the Son, and of the Holy Spirit, highlighting the triune nature of God.

5. **Feast of Corpus Christi**: Celebrated on the Thursday after Trinity Sunday, the Feast of Corpus Christi honors the real presence of the body and blood of Jesus Christ in the Eucharist. This feast underscores the importance of the Eucharist as the source and summit of our faith, inviting us to deepen our reverence and devotion to this sacrament.

Biblical Example: In John 6:51-58, Jesus speaks about the bread of life, stating that unless one eats his flesh and drinks his blood, they have no life in them, pointing to the sacramental nature of the Eucharist.

Special liturgical days are not merely historical commemorations but opportunities for personal reflection and spiritual renewal. They invite us to deepen our understanding of the mysteries of our faith and to draw closer to God through prayer and contemplation. As we celebrate these special days, let us be mindful of their significance and allow them to deepen our relationship with God and strengthen our commitment to living out the Gospel in our daily lives.

IV

Prayers and Devotions

As we delve into Part III of the Roman Catholic Daily and Sunday Missal 2024, we encounter a crucial aspect of our faith.

47

Prayer for the masses

prayers for the Mass. These prayers are not mere words; they are the means through which we communicate with God, offering Him our adoration, thanksgiving, petition, and contrition. They guide us through the sacred liturgy, helping us to participate fully and attentively in the mysteries unfolding before us.

Prayers for Mass
In the Catholic tradition, the Mass is the central act of worship, where the faithful gather to offer praise and thanksgiving to God. The prayers used in the Mass are carefully chosen to reflect the Church's beliefs and teachings, as well as to guide the faithful in their worship. These prayers are divided into several categories, each serving a specific purpose in the liturgy. Let us delve into each of these categories to understand their significance and the biblical foundations behind them:

1. Introductory Rites:

- The introductory rites mark the beginning of the Mass, preparing the faithful to enter into worship. This includes the Sign of the Cross, the Penitential Act, the Kyrie Eleison (Lord, have mercy), the Gloria, and the Opening Prayer (Collect).
- The Sign of the Cross is a gesture that recalls our baptism and expresses our belief in the Trinity. It is a reminder of God's presence with us, as Jesus said in Matthew 28:19, "Go therefore and make disciples of all nations, baptizing them in the name of the Father and of the Son and of the Holy Spirit."
- The Penitential Act acknowledges our sinfulness and the need for God's mercy. As stated in 1 John 1:9, "If we confess our sins, he who is faithful and just will forgive us our sins and cleanse us from all unrighteousness."
- The Kyrie Eleison is a plea for mercy, echoing the cry of the blind men in Matthew 20:30-31, "Lord, have mercy on us, Son of David!"
- The Gloria is a hymn of praise to God, echoing the angels' song in Luke 2:14, "Glory to God in the highest heaven, and on earth peace among those whom he favors!"
- The Opening Prayer (Collect) gathers the intentions of the faithful and presents them to God. It is a time to focus our hearts and minds on God's presence among us.

2. Liturgy of the Word:
   - The Liturgy of the Word consists of readings from the Old Testament, the Psalms, the New Testament, and the Gospel, followed by a homily and the Creed.
   - The readings are chosen to instruct and inspire the faithful, as Paul wrote in 2 Timothy 3:16-17, "All scripture is inspired by God and is useful for teaching, for reproof, for correction, and for training in righteousness, so that everyone who belongs to

God may be proficient, equipped for every good work."

- The homily is a reflection on the readings, helping the faithful to understand and apply them to their lives. This is in accordance with Titus 2:1, "But as for you, teach what is consistent with sound doctrine."

- The Creed is a statement of faith, affirming our belief in the core tenets of Christianity. As Paul wrote in Romans 10:9, "If you confess with your lips that Jesus is Lord and believe in your heart that God raised him from the dead, you will be saved."

3. Liturgy of the Eucharist:

- The Liturgy of the Eucharist is the central act of the Mass, where bread and wine are consecrated and become the body and blood of Christ.

- The Eucharistic Prayer, which includes the Preface, the Sanctus (Holy, Holy, Holy), the Institution Narrative, the Anamnesis (Memorial Acclamation), and the Doxology, is a prayer of thanksgiving and consecration.

- The words of institution, "This is my body... This is my blood," echo Jesus' words at the Last Supper in Matthew 26:26- 28, "While they were eating, Jesus took a loaf of bread, and after blessing it he broke it, gave it to the disciples, and said, 'Take, eat; this is my body.' Then he took a cup, and after giving thanks he gave it to them, saying, 'Drink from it, all of you; for this is my blood of the covenant, which is poured out for many for the forgiveness of sins.'"

- The Anamnesis recalls Christ's sacrifice on the cross and his resurrection, as Paul wrote in 1 Corinthians 11:26, "For as often as you eat this bread and drink the cup, you proclaim the Lord's death until he comes."

4. Concluding Rites:

- The concluding rites mark the end of the Mass and send forth the faithful to live out their faith in the world. This includes the Lord's Prayer, the Sign of Peace, the Breaking of the Bread, and the Final Blessing.
- The Lord's Prayer, also known as the Our Father, is a prayer taught by Jesus himself, as recorded in Matthew 6:9-13, "Pray then in this way: Our Father in heaven, hallowed be your name"
- The Sign of Peace is a gesture of reconciliation and unity, as Jesus said in Matthew 5:23-24, "So when you are offering your gift at the altar, if you remember that your brother or sister has something against you, leave your gift there before the altar and go; first be reconciled to your brother or sister, and then come and offer your gift."
- The Breaking of the Bread symbolizes the sharing of Christ's body and blood with the faithful, as Paul wrote in 1 Corinthians 10:16, "The cup of blessing that we bless, is it not a sharing in the blood of Christ? The bread that we break, is it not a sharing in the body of Christ?"
- The Final Blessing is a prayer for God's grace and protection, as Paul wrote in 2 Corinthians 13:14, "The grace of the Lord Jesus Christ, the love of God, and the communion of the Holy Spirit be with all of you."

In conclusion, the prayers for Mass are not just words spoken during worship, but a reflection of the beliefs and teachings of the Catholic Church, grounded in Scripture and tradition. They guide the faithful in their worship, deepen their understanding of the faith, and strengthen their relationship with God and one another.

48

Introductory Rites

The Introductory Rites mark the beginning of the Mass and serve to prepare the faithful to enter into the celebration with hearts and minds open to the Word of God and the Eucharistic sacrifice. These rites consist of several key elements:

1. **Entrance Procession**: The Mass begins with the entrance procession, during which the priest, deacon, and other ministers enter the church in a dignified manner, often accompanied by music. This procession symbolizes the journey of the faithful towards God and sets the tone for the worship that follows.

Biblical Example: In the Old Testament, we see processions being used in worship, such as when the Ark of the Covenant was brought to Jerusalem with great celebration and joy (2 Samuel 6:12-15).

2. **Sign of the Cross and Greeting**: The priest begins the Mass by

making the sign of the cross, invoking the name of the Father, and of the Son, and of the Holy Spirit. This act signifies our belief in the Triune God and our desire to unite ourselves with Him in worship. The priest then greets the people, expressing the Church's desire for God's grace and peace to be with them.

Biblical Example: In his letters, St. Paul often begins by invoking God's grace and peace upon the recipients (e.g., Romans 1:7; 1 Corinthians 1:3).

3. **Penitential Act**: Following the greeting, the Penitential Act is an opportunity for the faithful to acknowledge their sins and ask for God's mercy and forgiveness. This act prepares us to receive the Word of God with contrite hearts.

Biblical Example: King David's prayer of repentance in Psalm 51 serves as a model for seeking God's mercy and forgiveness.

4. Kyrie Eleison (Lord, Have Mercy): The congregation then joins in the Kyrie Eleison, a Greek prayer for mercy, sung or recited as a plea for God's compassion and forgiveness.

Biblical Example: In the Gospels, we see numerous examples of people crying out to Jesus for mercy, such as the blind beggar Bartimaeus (Mark 10:46-52).

5. **Gloria**: The Gloria is a hymn of praise to the Most Holy Trinity, glorifying God for His goodness and mercy. It is often omitted during Advent and Lent.

Biblical Example: The song of the angels at the birth of Jesus in Luke 2:14 is a form of Gloria, praising God and proclaiming peace on earth.

Overall, the Introductory Rites prepare us to enter into the mys- teries of the Mass by acknowledging our need for God's mercy, expressing our desire to praise and worship Him, and opening our hearts to receive His Word and Sacrament. Through these rites, we are reminded of our dependence on God and our need to continually seek His grace and forgiveness in our lives.

49

Liturgy of the Word

The Liturgy of the Word is a sacred and integral part of the Catholic Mass where the faithful are nourished and instructed by the Word of God. It is a time when the Scriptures are proclaimed, allowing us to encounter the living God in His Word. This part of the Mass is rooted in the Jewish tradition of reading from the Torah and the Prophets in the synagogue.

During the Liturgy of the Word, we listen attentively to readings from the Old Testament, the Psalms, the New Testament letters, and the Gospels. These readings are carefully selected and arranged in a way that reveals God's plan of salvation for humanity. The Responsorial Psalm allows us to respond to God's Word in a spirit of prayer and contemplation.

One of the key aspects of the Liturgy of the Word is the homily, where the priest or deacon offers a reflection on the readings. The homily is meant to help the faithful understand the Scrip- tures in the context of their daily lives and to apply its teachings to their own journey of faith. The homilist should draw upon the richness of Catholic tradition, the teachings of the Church Fathers, and the insights of modern scholarship to provide a meaningful and relevant message.

Throughout the Liturgy of the Word, we are reminded of the importance of Scripture in the life of the Church. As St. Paul writes in his letter to Timothy, "All Scripture is inspired by God and is useful for teaching, for reproof, for correction, and for training in righteousness, so that everyone who belongs to God may be proficient, equipped for every good work" (2 Timothy 3:16-17). The Word of God has the power to transform our hearts and minds, leading us closer to God and His divine will for us.

50

Liturgy of the Eucharist

The Liturgy of the Eucharist is the central and most sacred part of the Catholic Mass, where the bread and wine are consecrated and become the body and blood of Christ. This part of the Mass is based on the Last Supper, where Jesus instituted the Eucharist as a memorial of His sacrifice on the cross.

The Liturgy of the Eucharist begins with the presentation of the gifts of bread and wine, which symbolize the offering of ourselves to God. The priest then prays over the gifts, invoking the Holy Spirit to transform them into the body and blood of Christ. This moment is a profound expression of our faith in the real presence of Christ in the Eucharist.

The Eucharistic Prayer, which includes the consecration of the bread and wine, is the high point of the Liturgy of the Eucharist. During this prayer, the priest recalls the words of Jesus at the Last Supper and invokes the power of the Holy Spirit to make

Christ present in the Eucharist. This prayer is a solemn and sacred moment, and the faithful are called to participate in it with reverence and awe.

After the consecration, the faithful receive Holy Communion, partaking of the body and blood of Christ. This act of receiving Communion is a profound expression of our unity with Christ and with one another. As St. Paul writes in his first letter to the Corinthians, "Because there is one bread, we who are many are one body, for we all partake of the one bread" (1 Corinthians 10:17).

51

Concluding Rites

The Concluding Rites of the Mass bring the celebration to a close and send forth the faithful to live out their faith in the world. This part of the Mass includes the final blessing, the dismissal, and the procession out of the church.

The final blessing is a prayer invoking God's grace and protec- tion upon the faithful. It is a reminder of God's presence in our lives and His desire to bless us with His love and mercy. The priest, acting in the person of Christ, imparts this blessing on behalf of the Church.

The dismissal is a symbolic sending forth of the faithful to proclaim the Gospel in their daily lives. It is a commissioning to go out into the world and be witnesses to the love and truth of Christ. As Jesus said to His disciples before His ascension, "Go therefore and make disciples of all nations, baptizing them in the name of the Father and of the Son and of the Holy Spirit" (Matthew 28:19).

As we conclude the Mass and go forth into the world, we are reminded of our mission as Christians to be a light to the world and to share the good news of salvation with all those we encounter. The Mass is not just a Sunday obligation but a source of grace and strength that empowers us to live out our faith in the world.

V

Devotions and Litanies

Devotions and litanies are essential aspects of Catholic prayer life, offering a structured and meaningful way to deepen one's relationship with God. These prayers, often rich in tradition and history, provide a framework for personal reflection, meditation, and supplication. They help believers express their faith, seek intercession, and cultivate a spirit of devotion. In this section, we will explore various devotions and litanies commonly practiced in the Catholic Church, their significance.

52

Rosary

The Rosary is a cherished Catholic devotion that combines prayer and meditation on the life of Jesus Christ through the intercession of the Blessed Virgin Mary. It is a powerful tool for spiritual growth and a source of great comfort and peace for believers. The word "rosary" comes from the Latin "rosarium," which means "rose garden" or "garland of roses," symbolizing the offering of prayers as a spiritual bouquet to Mary.

The Rosary is composed of a series of prayers, including the Apostles' Creed, the Our Father, the Hail Mary, and the Glory Be. These prayers are divided into decades, each focusing on a different mystery from the life of Jesus and Mary. The traditional Mysteries of the Rosary are divided into four sets: the Joyful Mysteries, the Sorrowful Mysteries, the Glorious Mysteries, and the Luminous Mysteries.

1. **Apostles' Creed**: The Rosary begins with the Apostles' Creed, a statement of faith that summarizes the core beliefs of Christianity. By reciting this creed, Catholics

affirm their belief in God, Jesus Christ, the Holy Spirit, the Church, and the forgiveness of sins.

2. **Our Father:** The Our Father, also known as the Lord's Prayer, is a prayer taught by Jesus to his disciples. It acknowledges God as our Father in heaven and asks for His will to be done on earth as it is in heaven. By praying the Our Father, Catholics express their dependence on God and seek His guidance and provision.

3. **HailMary:** TheHailMaryisaprayerthathonorsMary,the mother of Jesus. It consists of two parts: the first part is a greeting by the Angel Gabriel at the Annunciation, and the second part is a request for Mary's intercession. Catholics believe that Mary is a powerful intercessor who can bring their prayers to Jesus.

4. **Glory Be:** The Glory Be is a short prayer of praise to the Holy Trinity - Father, Son, and Holy Spirit. It acknowl- edges the greatness and majesty of God and expresses gratitude for His blessings.

The Mysteries of the Rosary are meditated upon during the recitation of the prayers, allowing Catholics to reflect on key moments in the lives of Jesus and Mary. Each set of mysteries offers spiritual lessons and insights into the mysteries of faith.

- **Joyful Mysteries**: These mysteries focus on the joyful events surrounding the birth and early life of Jesus, including the Annunciation, the Visitation, the Nativity, the Presentation in the Temple, and the Finding of the Child Jesus in the Temple. These mysteries highlight themes of humility, obedience, and the joy of salvation.

- **Sorrowful Mysteries**: The Sorrowful Mysteries reflect on the suffering and death of Jesus, including the Agony in the Garden, the Scourging at the Pillar, the Crowning with Thorns, the Carrying of the Cross, and the Crucifixion. These mysteries invite believers to contemplate the depth of Jesus' love and sacrifice for humanity.

- **Glorious Mysteries**: The Glorious Mysteries focus on the triumph of Jesus and Mary, including the Resurrection, the Ascension, the Descent of the Holy Spirit at Pentecost, the Assumption of Mary into Heaven, and the Coronation of Mary as Queen of Heaven and Earth. These mysteries inspire hope and confidence in the victory of Christ over sin and death.

- **Luminous Mysteries**: Instituted by Pope John Paul II in 2002, the Luminous Mysteries highlight key moments in the public ministry of Jesus, including His Baptism in the Jordan, His self- revelation at the Wedding Feast of Cana, His proclamation of the Kingdom of God, His Transfiguration, and His institution of the Eucharist. These mysteries deepen our understanding of Jesus' mission and invite us to follow Him more closely.

Throughout the centuries, the Rosary has been a source of spiritual strength and consolation for countless Catholics. It is a prayer that can be recited individually or in groups, and it is often used in times of personal need or communal prayer. The repetition of the prayers and the meditation on the mysteries help to quiet the mind and open the heart to God's presence.

Biblical Example: In Luke 1:26-38, the Angel Gabriel announces to Mary that she will conceive and bear a son, Jesus. Mary's response, "Behold, I am the handmaid of the Lord; let it be done to me according to your word," (Luke 1:38) exemplifies her humility and obedience to God's will, which are virtues reflected in the Joyful Mysteries of the Rosary.

53

The Divine Mercy Chaplet

The Divine Mercy Chaplet and the Litany of the Saints are two powerful prayers in the Catholic tradition, each with its own rich history and significance. Let us delve into each of these devotions, exploring their meanings, origins, and how they are prayed.

The Divine Mercy Chaplet:
The Divine Mercy Chaplet is a prayer that focuses on the mercy of God, particularly as revealed through Jesus Christ. It originated from the visions of Saint Faustina Kowalska, a Polish nun who reported visions and conversations with Jesus in the 1930s. In these visions, Jesus emphasized the importance of trust in His mercy and the need to pray for God's mercy on the whole world.

The Chaplet is typically prayed using a set of rosary beads and consists of a specific pattern of prayers. It begins with the Sign of the Cross, followed by the recitation of the Our Father, the Hail Mary, and the Apostles' Creed. Then, on the large bead before each decade, the following prayer is said: "Eternal Father, I offer you the Body and Blood, Soul and Divinity of Your dearly beloved Son, Our Lord Jesus Christ, in atonement for our sins and those of the whole world."

After each decade (a set of 10 beads), the following prayer is said on the small beads: "For the sake of His sorrowful Passion, have mercy on us and on the whole world." The Chaplet concludes with a series of prayers, including the prayer, "Holy God, Holy Mighty One, Holy Immortal One, have mercy on us and on the whole world."

The Divine Mercy Chaplet is a powerful prayer of intercession, asking God to have mercy on us and on the whole world. It is a reminder of God's infinite mercy and His desire to forgive us if we come to Him with contrite hearts.

The Litany of the Saints:

The Litany of the Saints is a prayer that invokes the intercession of the saints. It is a liturgical prayer used in various Christian traditions, including the Catholic Church. The litany is a form of prayer where a series of petitions are made, often followed by a repeated response. In the case of the Litany of the Saints, the petitions are addressed to specific saints, asking for their prayers and intercession.

The Litany of the Saints has a long history in the Catholic Church, dating back to the early centuries of Christianity. It is often used in liturgical celebrations, especially during the Easter Vigil and the ordination of priests. The litany includes invocations to many saints, including the Virgin Mary, the apostles, martyrs, and other holy men and women recognized by the Church.

One of the key themes of the Litany of the Saints is the commu- nion of saints, which is the belief that all the faithful, both living and dead, are united in Christ. By invoking the intercession of the saints, believers express their belief in the power of prayer and the solidarity of the Church across time and space.

Both the Divine Mercy Chaplet and the Litany of the Saints are prayers that reflect the Catholic belief in the communion of saints and the power of intercessory prayer. They are prayers that remind us of God's mercy and the support of the saints in our spiritual journey.

54

Others devotions and litanies

In the Catholic tradition, devotions and litanies play a significant role in deepening one's spiritual life and fostering a
closer relationship with God. These practices are not
mandatory but are encouraged as aids to prayer and
reflection. They help Catholics express their faith, seek
intercession from the saints, and meditate on the mysteries
of the faith. Here, we will explore some of the key devotions
and litanies practiced by Catholics around the world.

1. The Rosary: The Rosary is a beloved Catholic prayer that
focuses on the life of Jesus and Mary. It consists of
meditations on the mysteries of the faith, divided into sets of
five decades, each preceded by the Our Father and followed
by the Glory Be. The Rosary is a powerful tool for meditation
and contemplation, helping believers to deepen their
understanding of the life, death, and resurrection of Jesus.
  Biblical Example: The Hail Mary prayer, a central part of the
Rosary, is based on two passages from the Bible: "Hail, full of
grace, the Lord is with you" (Luke 1:28) and "Blessed are you

148

among women, and blessed is the fruit of your womb" (Luke 1:42).

2. DivineMercyChaplet: TheDivineMercyChapletisa devotion that focuses on God's mercy, particularly as revealed to St. Faustina Kowalska. It involves the recitation of prayers, including the Our Father, the Hail Mary, and the Apostles' Creed, as well as a series of prayers specifically focused on seeking God's mercy for oneself and others.

Biblical Example: The Chaplet reflects the biblical message of God's abundant mercy, as seen in passages such as Psalm 103:8, which says, "The Lord is merciful and gracious, slow to anger and abounding in steadfast love."

3. Litany of the Saints: A litany is a form of prayer that consists of a series of invocations or petitions, often addressed to God, Mary, or the saints. The Litany of the Saints is a powerful prayer in which the faithful call upon the saints to intercede for them. It is often used in the liturgy, especially during the Easter Vigil and the ordination of priests.

Biblical Example: The concept of invoking the saints is rooted in the Bible, where we see examples of believers asking for the intercession of others, such as when Paul asks his fellow Christians to pray for him (Romans 15:30).

4. Other Devotions and Litanies: In addition to the Rosary, Divine Mercy Chaplet, and Litany of the Saints, there are numer- ous other devotions and litanies practiced by Catholics. These include prayers to specific saints for their intercession, such as the St. Jude Novena for hopeless cases, the St. Anthony Novena for lost items, and the St. Joseph Novena for employment and housing needs. There are also litanies dedicated to specific aspects of the faith, such as the Litany of the Sacred Heart of Jesus and the Litany of the Blessed Virgin Mary.

Biblical Example: These devotions and litanies are based on the belief in the communion of saints, as described in Hebrews 12:1, which says, "Therefore, since we are surrounded by so great a cloud of witnesses, let us also lay aside every weight, and sin which clings so closely, and let us run with endurance the race that is set before us."

In conclusion, devotions and litanies are an integral part of Catholic spirituality, providing believers with tools for prayer, meditation, and seeking intercession from the saints. These practices help Catholics deepen their relationship with God and grow in their faith.

VI

Appendices

55

Liturgical Calendar

The liturgical calendar is a sacred and structured framework that guides the worship and spiritual life of the Catholic Church. It is a cyclical calendar that revolves around the life of Christ, celebrating various aspects of His life, ministry, and salvific work. Understanding the liturgical calendar is essential for Catholics as it helps us enter more deeply into the mysteries of our faith and unite ourselves with the Church's universal prayer.

Explanation of the Liturgical Year

The liturgical year, also known as the Christian year or church year, is divided into different seasons, each with its own focus and theme. These seasons help us to meditate on the key events in the life of Christ and the Church, and they invite us to enter into the mysteries of our salvation.

The liturgical year begins with the season of Advent, a time of joyful expectation and preparation for the coming of Christ. During Advent, we reflect on the prophecies of the Old Testament and prepare our hearts to welcome the Messiah.

Christmas is the celebration of the birth of Jesus Christ, the Son of God, who came into the world to save us from sin and death. It is a time of great joy and hope as we celebrate the Incarnation and the beginning of our salvation.

Following Christmas, we enter the season of Ordinary Time, which is a time of growth and maturation in our faith. During Ordinary Time, we reflect on the teachings of Jesus and strive to live as His disciples in the world.

Lent is a season of penance and preparation for Easter. It is a time of prayer, fasting, and almsgiving as we prepare to celebrate the Paschal Mystery of Christ's passion, death, and resurrection.

Easter is the celebration of Christ's victory over sin and death. It is the culmination of the liturgical year and the foundation of our faith. During the Easter season, we rejoice in the resurrection of Jesus and the promise of eternal life.

After Easter, we enter another period of Ordinary Time, during which we continue to reflect on the teachings of Jesus and grow in our discipleship.

The liturgical year concludes with the feast of Christ the King, which celebrates Jesus Christ as the King of the Universe. It is a reminder that Christ is the center of our lives and the source of our hope.

Table of Liturgical Seasons and Colors

Each season of the liturgical year is associated with a specific liturgical color, which is used in the vestments and decorations of the church. These colors have symbolic meanings and help to convey the mood and theme of each season.

- **Advent**: The color for Advent is purple, which symbolizes penance and preparation. It is a reminder to us to prepare our hearts for the coming of Christ.

- **Christmas:** The color for Christmas is white or gold, which symbolizes joy and purity. It reflects the joy of the Incarnation and the purity of Christ.

- **Ordinary Time**: The color for Ordinary Time is green, which symbolizes hope and growth. It is a reminder to us to continue growing in our faith and discipleship.

- **Lent**: The color for Lent is purple, which symbolizes penance and repentance. It is a reminder to us of the need to repent of our sins and turn back to God.

- **Easter**: The color for Easter is white or gold, which symbolizes joy and victory. It reflects the joy of Christ's resurrection and the victory of life over death.

- **Solemnities and Feasts**: For solemnities and feasts, the color is usually white or gold, symbolizing the importance and joy of the celebration.

- Memorials and Optional Memorials: For memorials and optional memorials, the color is usually green, unless the feast has its own specific color.

The liturgical colors serve as a visual reminder of the significance of each season and help us to enter more deeply into the mysteries of our faith. They invite us to reflect on the themes of each season and to allow God's grace to transform us more fully into the image of Christ.

56

Glossary of Liturgical Terms

In the Roman Catholic Church, the liturgy is rich with symbol- ism and tradition, often using specific terms and phrases that may be unfamiliar to those new to the faith or even to long-time practitioners. This glossary aims to provide clarity on some of the key terms and phrases used in the liturgy, helping to deepen one's understanding and appreciation of the Mass and other liturgical celebrations.

1. **Liturgy**: The public worship of the Church, including the celebration of the Mass, the Liturgy of the Hours, and other sacraments and rites.
2. **Mass**: The central act of Catholic worship, where the Eucharist is celebrated. It is divided into two main parts: the Liturgy of the Word and the Liturgy of the Eucharist.
3. **Eucharist**: AlsoknownasHolyCommunion,theEucharist is the sacrament in which Catholics believe the bread and wine become the body and blood of Jesus Christ.
4. **Sacrament**: A visible sign of God's grace, instituted by Christ and entrusted to the Church. The seven sacraments

are Baptism, Confirmation, Eucharist, Penance, Anointing of the Sick, Holy Orders, and Matrimony.

5. **Liturgy of the Word**: The first main part of the Mass, during which readings from the Bible are proclaimed and reflected upon.

6. **Liturgy of the Eucharist**: The second main part of the Mass, during which the bread and wine are consecrated and become the body and blood of Christ.

7. **Lectionary**: The book containing the readings from the Bible used at Mass.

8. **Missal**: The book containing the prayers, readings, and instructions for the celebration of Mass.

9. **Sacramentary**: An older term for the missal, referring specifically to the book containing the prayers used by the priest at Mass.

10. **Altar**: The table at the front of the church where the Eucharist is celebrated.

11. **Chalice**: Thecupusedtoholdthewinethatbecomesthe blood of Christ during Mass.

12. **Ciborium**: The vessel used to hold the consecrated hosts (the body of Christ) for distribution during Communion.

13. **Ambo**: Thepodiumorlecternfromwhichthereadingsare proclaimed during Mass.

14. **Tabernacle**: The locked box or cabinet where the consecrated hosts are kept for adoration and distribution to the sick.

15. **Sacristy**: Theroominthechurchwherethepriestprepares for Mass and where liturgical items are stored.

16. **Vestments**: The special clothing worn by the priest and other ministers during Mass, including the alb, stole, and chasuble.

17. **Liturgical Colors**: The colors used for the priest's vestments and other decorations in the church, which change depending on the liturgical season or feast day.

18. **Advent**: The season of preparation for Christmas, beginning four Sundays before Christmas Day.

19. **Lent**: The season of preparation for Easter, beginning on Ash Wednesday and lasting for 40 days (excluding Sundays).

20. **Triduum**: The three-day period leading up to Easter Sunday, including Holy Thursday, Good Friday, and Holy Saturday.

Understanding these terms can enhance one's experience of the Mass and other liturgical celebrations, deepening one's appreciation for the rich tradition and symbolism of Catholic worship. As St. Paul writes in Colossians 3:16, "Let the word of Christ dwell in you richly, teaching and admonishing one another in all wisdom, singing psalms and hymns and spiritual songs, with thankfulness in your hearts to God."

57

Index of Readings and Prayers

The Index of Readings and Prayers is an essential component of the Roman Catholic Daily and Sunday Missal 2024. It serves as a comprehensive guide, enabling worshippers to easily locate specific readings and prayers within the Missal. This index is particularly valuable for those who wish to deepen their understanding of the liturgy and follow along with the Mass more attentively.

Alphabetical Index of Readings

The alphabetical index of readings provides a list of all the biblical passages included in the Missal, arranged alphabetically by book, chapter, and verse. This index allows worshippers to quickly locate a specific reading by referencing its title or a keyword from the passage. For example, if one wishes to find the reading about the Good Samaritan, they can simply look up "Samaritan" in the index and find Luke 10:25-37.

Alphabetical Index of Prayers

Similarly, the alphabetical index of prayers offers a convenient way to find specific prayers included in the Missal. This index lists prayers by their titles or keywords, allowing individuals to easily locate prayers for particular intentions or occasions. For instance, if someone is seeking the Prayer of St. Francis, they can find it by looking up "Francis" in the index and locating the prayer under its title.

Importance of the Index

The index of readings and prayers plays a crucial role in enhancing the liturgical experience for worshippers. It enables them to navigate the Missal with ease, ensuring that they can participate fully in the Mass and engage more deeply with the Word of God and the prayers of the Church. By providing a clear and organized reference guide, the index helps to facilitate a more meaningful and enriching worship experience.

Biblical Example: Psalm 119:105

The importance of the index can be likened to the role of light in guiding our path. Just as Psalm 119:105 proclaims, "Your word is a lamp to my feet and a light to my path," the index serves as a guiding light, illuminating the way for worshippers as they navigate the Missal. It ensures that they can find their desired readings and prayers with ease, allowing them to draw closer to God through His Word and the prayers of the Church.

Conclusion

In conclusion, the Index of Readings and Prayers is a valuable resource within the Roman Catholic Daily and Sunday Missal 2024. It provides worshippers with a convenient means of locating specific biblical passages and prayers, enhancing their ability to participate fully in the Mass and deepen their spiritual experience. Through its organized and accessible format, the index serves as a guiding light, leading worshippers to a deeper encounter with God's Word and the rich tradition of prayer in the Catholic Church.

58

About the Roman Catholic Church

The Roman Catholic Church, often simply called the Catholic Church, is a rich and complex institution with a long and storied history, deep-rooted beliefs, and a wide array of practices that have evolved over centuries. To truly understand the Catholic Church, one must delve into its history, explore its core beliefs, and examine its key practices. In this exploration, we will look at each of these aspects in detail, drawing on biblical examples where appropriate to illustrate key points.

History of the Catholic Church:

The history of the Catholic Church is a tapestry woven with the threads of time, stretching back to the very foundations of Christianity. The Catholic Church traces its origins to Jesus Christ, who founded the Church upon the apostle Peter, as described in the Gospel of Matthew:

"And I tell you, you are Peter, and on this rock I will build my church, and the gates of Hades will not prevail against it." (Matthew 16:18)

From these humble beginnings, the Church grew and spread

throughout the Roman Empire, facing persecution and challenges along the way. The early Church Fathers, such as Ignatius of Antioch and Clement of Rome, played a crucial role in shaping the early Church and its teachings.

As the Church expanded, it became a central institution in medieval Europe, exerting influence over both spiritual and temporal affairs. The crowning of Charlemagne as Holy Roman Emperor in 800 AD marked a significant moment in the Church's history, symbolizing the close relationship between the Church and European rulers.

The Church weathered numerous challenges over the centuries, including the Great Schism of 1054, which split the Church into the Western (Catholic) and Eastern (Orthodox) branches, and the Protestant Reformation of the 16th century, which led to further divisions within Western Christianity. Despite these challenges, the Catholic Church has remained a vibrant and influential force in the world, continuing to spread the message of Christ to all corners of the globe.

Beliefs of the Catholic Church:
At the heart of Catholic belief is the affirmation of the Nicene Creed, a statement of faith that summarizes the core tenets of Christianity. This creed declares belief in one God, the Father Almighty, creator of heaven and earth, of all things visible and invisible, and in Jesus Christ, His only Son, our Lord, who was conceived by the Holy Spirit, born of the Virgin Mary, suffered under Pontius Pilate, was crucified, died, and was buried; He descended into hell; on the third day He rose again from the dead; He ascended into heaven, and is seated at the right hand

of God the Father Almighty; from there He will come to judge the living and the dead.

The Catholic Church also upholds the authority of the Pope, who is regarded as the successor of Peter and the Vicar of Christ on earth. This belief is based on the words of Jesus to Peter in the Gospel of Matthew:

"And I tell you, you are Peter, and on this rock I will build my church, and the gates of Hades will not prevail against it. I will give you the keys of the kingdom of heaven, and whatever you bind on earth will be bound in heaven, and whatever you loose on earth will be loosed in heaven." (Matthew 16:18-19) The Catholic Church teaches that the Pope, as the Bishop of Rome, holds a primacy of jurisdiction over the entire Church, and that he is infallible when defining matters of faith and morals ex cathedra (from the chair of Peter).

Practices of the Catholic Church:

Central to Catholic practice is the celebration of the sacraments, which are visible signs of God's grace. The Catholic Church recognizes seven sacraments: Baptism, Confirmation, Eucharist, Penance (Reconciliation), Anointing of the Sick, Holy Orders, and Matrimony. These sacraments are believed to confer grace upon the recipient, strengthening them in their Christian journey.

The celebration of the Mass is also a central practice of the Catholic Church. The Mass is a reenactment of the Last Supper, where Jesus instituted the Eucharist. During the Mass, Catholics believe that the bread and wine become the body and blood of Christ, a belief known as the doctrine of Transubstantiation.

The Catholic Church also places a strong emphasis on prayer, both communal and individual. The Rosary, a form of prayer that meditates on the life of Christ through the recitation of prayers and the repetition of certain prayers, such as the Hail Mary and the Our Father, is a popular devotional practice among Catholics.

In conclusion, the Roman Catholic Church is a complex and multifaceted institution with a rich history, deep-rooted beliefs, and a wide array of practices. Its history stretches back to the time of Christ, and its beliefs are rooted in the teachings of the apostles and the early Church Fathers. Its practices, including the celebration of the sacraments and the Mass, are central to the spiritual life of Catholics around the world. Through its history, beliefs, and practices, the Catholic Church continues to be a vibrant and influential force in the world, spreading the message of Christ to all who will listen.

59

How to Live Your Faith Daily

Living a Catholic life is about more than just attending Mass on Sundays. It's about embodying the teachings of Christ in every aspect of our daily lives. Here are some practical tips for living a Catholic life:

1. **Prayer**: Start and end your day with prayer. Jesus often withdrew to pray alone (Luke 5:16), showing us the importance of personal prayer. Pray the Lord's Prayer (Matthew 6:9-13) and the Rosary regularly for spiritual growth.

2. **Scripture Reading**: Read the Bible daily to understand God's word and strengthen your faith. The Bible is a lamp for our feet and a light on our path (Psalm 119:105).

3. **Mass Attendance**: Attend Mass regularly, not just on Sundays but also on weekdays if possible. The Eucharist is the source and summit of our faith (CCC 1324) and strengthens us to live as faithful disciples of Christ.

4. **Receiving the Sacraments**: Regularly receive the sacraments of Reconciliation and Holy Communion. Confession cleanses us from sin, and the Eucharist nourishes us

spiritually.

5. **Christian Community**: Participate in your parish community. Build relationships with fellow Catholics to support and encourage one another in your faith journey (Hebrews 10:24-25).

6. **WorksofMercy**: Practicethecorporalandspiritualworks of mercy (Matthew 25:31-46). Feed the hungry, give drink to the thirsty, clothe the naked, visit the sick and imprisoned, and comfort the sorrowful.

7. **Living Virtuously**: Strive to live a virtuous life. Practice the cardinal virtues of prudence, justice, fortitude, and temperance, as well as the theological virtues of faith, hope, and charity (1 Corinthians 13:13).

8. **Avoiding Sin**: Be aware of your weaknesses and avoid occasions of sin. Pray for the strength to resist temptation (1 Corinthians 10:13).

9. **Fasting and Abstinence**: Fast and abstain from meat on Fridays as a penitential practice (Mark 2:18-20).

10. **Stewardship**: Use your time, talents, and treasure wisely for the glory of God. Be a good steward of God's gifts (1 Peter 4:10).

11. **Seeking God's Will:** Regularly discern God's will for your life through prayer and reflection. Trust in the Lord with all your heart and lean not on your own understanding (Proverbs 3:5-6).

12. **Forgiveness**: Forgive others as God has forgiven you (Ephesians 4:32). Let go of resentment and anger, and seek reconciliation.

Living a Catholic life is a journey that requires daily effort and commitment. By following these practical tips, you can grow in your relationship with God and live as a true disciple of Christ.

VII

Conclusion

60

Conclusion

As we conclude our journey through the Roman Catholic Daily and Sunday Missal 2024, it is fitting to reflect on its significance and encourage all faithful to embrace its riches for a deeper spiritual life.

Firstly, the Missal is not just a book; it is a treasury of our faith, containing the prayers, readings, and rituals that guide us through the liturgical year. Each page is imbued with the wisdom and beauty of our Catholic tradition, inviting us to enter more fully into the mystery of our salvation.

In 2 Timothy 3:16-17, St. Paul reminds us that "All Scripture is inspired by God and is useful for teaching, for reproof, for correction, and for training in righteousness, so that everyone who belongs to God may be proficient, equipped for every good work." The Missal, by providing us with the daily readings of Scripture, helps us to grow in our understanding of God's Word and its application to our lives.

Moreover, the Missal is a guide for prayer, leading us in the worship of God and the offering of ourselves to Him. In Psalm 95:6, we are exhorted to "Come, let us bow down in worship, let us kneel before the Lord our Maker." Daily Mass attendance, as encouraged by the Missal, allows us to fulfill this call to worship and draw closer to God.

Attending Mass regularly is not just a duty; it is a privilege and a source of great grace. In the Gospel of John (6:54), Jesus tells us, "Whoever eats my flesh and drinks my blood has eternal life, and I will raise them up at the last day." The Eucharist, the center of our Catholic faith, is celebrated at every Mass, offering us the opportunity to receive Jesus into our hearts and be nourished by His Body and Blood.

Furthermore, the Missal invites us to participate actively in the liturgy, not as passive spectators but as engaged members of the Body of Christ. In 1 Corinthians 12:27, St. Paul writes, "Now you are the body of Christ, and each one of you is a part of it." Our active participation in the Mass, through singing, responding to prayers, and listening attentively to the readings, helps to build up the Church and deepen our communion with one another.

In conclusion, the Roman Catholic Daily and Sunday Missal 2024 is a precious gift to the Church, offering us a guide to a richer, more vibrant spiritual life. Let us embrace its teachings and prayers with gratitude, and let us commit ourselves to regular Mass attendance, so that we may be nourished by the Word of God and the Sacrament of the Eucharist. As we journey through the liturgical year, may the Missal be a source of inspiration and strength, leading us ever closer to God and His kingdom. Amen.

61

Encouragement for Daily Mass Attendance and Participation

Encouraging daily Mass attendance and active participation is a fundamental aspect of the Catholic faith. The Mass is the source and summit of our Christian life, where we encounter the living Christ in the Eucharist and are nourished by His Word. Daily Mass offers a unique opportunity to deepen our relationship with God and grow in holiness. Here are some key points to consider in encouraging daily Mass attendance and participation:

1. **The Importance of the Eucharist**: Daily Mass allows us to receive the body and blood of Christ more frequently, strengthening our spiritual life and providing us with the grace we need to live as faithful disciples. Jesus Himself said, "I am the living bread that came down from heaven. Whoever eats of this bread will live forever; and the bread that I will give for the life of the world is my flesh" (John 6:51).
2. **The Power of Communal Worship**: Gathering with fellow

believers for Mass reminds us that we are part of the Body of Christ, the Church. St. Paul encourages us to "not neglect to meet together, as is the habit of some, but encourage one another, and all the more as you see the Day approaching" (Hebrews 10:25). Daily Mass strengthens our sense of community and unity with other believers.

3. Spiritual Nourishment and Growth: Daily Mass provides us with spiritual nourishment through the Word of God and the Eucharist. Jesus said, "Man shall not live by bread alone, but by every word that comes from the mouth of God" (Matthew 4:4). Attending Mass daily helps us grow in our understanding of Scripture and deepens our spiritual life.

4. **Witness to Faith**: By attending Massdaily, webear witness to our faith in Christ and His Church. Our commitment to daily Mass can inspire others to take their faith more seriously and can be a powerful testimony to the world of the transformative power of the Gospel.

5. Opportunity for Repentance and Conversion: Daily Mass provides us with the opportunity to repent of our sins and receive God's mercy and forgiveness. Through the penitential rite and the reception of the Eucharist, we are strengthened in our resolve to live according to God's will.

6. A Daily Encounter with Christ: Each Mass is a unique encounter with the living Christ. In the Eucharist, Jesus is truly present, body, blood, soul, and divinity. As we receive Him in Communion, we are united with Him in a profound and intimate way.

7. DeepeningOurRelationshipwithMary: DailyMassoften includes the recitation of the Angelus or other Marian prayers, deepening our relationship with the Mother of

177

God. Mary is our model of faith and obedience, and through her intercession, we can grow closer to her Son.

8. **Growing in Holiness**: Daily Mass is a means of growing in holiness and conforming our lives more closely to the example of Christ. As we receive the grace of the sacraments and hear God's Word proclaimed, we are empowered to live as faithful disciples in our daily lives.

In conclusion, daily Mass attendance and participation are essential aspects of the Catholic faith. It is through the Mass that we encounter Christ, receive His grace, and are strengthened in our journey of faith. I encourage you to make attending daily Mass a priority in your life, and may God bless you abundantly as you seek to grow closer to Him through this sacred practice.

Manufactured by Amazon.ca
Bolton, ON